Counterfeit Spirituality

COUNTERFEIT
SPIRITUALITY

EXPOSING THE

BRYAN MERCIER

Our Sunday Visitor
Huntington, Indiana

Nihil Obstat
Msgr. Michael Heintz, Ph.D.
Censor Librorum

Imprimatur
✠ Kevin C. Rhoades
Bishop of Fort Wayne-South Bend
October 25, 2019

The *Nihil Obstat* and *Imprimatur* are official declarations that a book is free from doctrinal or moral error. It is not implied that those who have granted the *Nihil Obstat* and *Imprimatur* agree with the contents, opinions, or statements expressed.

Except where noted, the Scripture citations used in this work are taken from the *Revised Standard Version of the Bible — Second Catholic Edition* (Ignatius Edition), copyright © 1965, 1966, 2006 National Council of the Churches of Christ in the United States of America. Used by permission. All rights reserved.

English translation of the *Catechism of the Catholic Church* for use in the United States of America copyright © 1994, United States Catholic Conference, Inc. — Libreria Editrice Vaticana. English translation of the *Catechism of the Catholic Church: Modifications from the Editio Typica* copyright © 1997, United States Catholic Conference, Inc. — Libreria Editrice Vaticana.

Every reasonable effort has been made to determine copyright holders of excerpted materials and to secure permissions as needed. If any copyrighted materials have been inadvertently used in this work without proper credit being given in one form or another, please notify Our Sunday Visitor in writing so that future printings of this work may be corrected accordingly.

Our Sunday Visitor Publishing Division
Our Sunday Visitor, Inc.
200 Noll Plaza
Huntington, IN 46750
1-800-348-2440

ISBN: 978-1-68192-301-7 (Inventory No. T1975)
1. RELIGION—Spirituality. 2. RELIGION—Cults. 3. RELIGION—Christianity—Catholic.

eISBN: 978-1-68192-302-4
LCCN: 2019930317

Cover design: Lindsey Riesen
Cover art: Shutterstock
Interior design: Lindsey Riesen

PRINTED IN THE UNITED STATES OF AMERICA

*Dedicated to the Lord Jesus Christ
for his kingdom and his glory*

CONTENTS

PREFACE
SPOTTING THE FAKES

B eware of counterfeits! Did you know that bankers are experts in identifying counterfeit money? Whereas some counterfeit bills are poorly created and easy to spot, many counterfeits are almost indistinguishable from the real thing. Most people cannot see or feel the difference between the genuine and the counterfeit, but bankers can spot a fake simply by touching the bills. Even though the real and the fake are almost identical, there are differences that can be detected by a person with the proper training. It always begins by knowing the real thing.

As one journalist confirmed with a bank executive: "Federal agents don't learn to spot counterfeit money by studying the counterfeits. They study genuine bills until they master the look of the real thing. Then when they see the bogus money they recognize it."[1] That is precisely how it is with our Faith. Only through a deep knowledge and understanding of the truth will we be able to recognize counterfeit teachings and practices when they arise. And there are many counterfeits!

Since the 1960s, tidal waves of false spiritual practices have flooded the Catholic Church and the lives of many Catholics, especially in the West. After Vatican II, some questioned the Catholic Church's teachings and authority. What began with questions ended with thousands of Catholics, even priests and nuns, abandoning the Faith and sometimes accepting other religious beliefs in its place. Many who remained in the Catholic

Church experimented and accepted other beliefs, even if those beliefs were against God and the Church.

As Donna Steichen narrates in her book *Ungodly Rage*, "Many of those who ceased to kneel for prayer began to substitute yoga postures, T'ai Chi, 'New Age' spiritualism or circumstances, widdershins, around a smoking cauldron. They sought 'empowerment' in the ancient 'wisdom' of Eastern monism, 'goddess' paganism, dubious 'Native American traditions,' voodoo, witchcraft, or the animist 'spirits' of the newly invented earth religions. Some who denied the existence of angels found New Age channeling and spirit guides credible."[2]

These beliefs, and many others, have entered the Catholic Church and have been passed down to unsuspecting people. Sadly, many beliefs and teachings that appear genuine are, in fact, bogus. As we will see throughout this book, many people who fall prey to these beliefs suffer greatly as a result. Just as counterfeit money brings trouble to the person who uses it, so, too, counterfeit spirituality leads souls astray and brings with it many bad consequences. True spirituality leads souls to God and to heaven, but counterfeit spirituality draws souls away from both and is detrimental to the life of the Church. Thus, it is of paramount importance that Christians be able to recognize the differences and detect the frauds, especially when the counterfeit spirituality is promoted by fellow Christians.

Perhaps someone you love is entrenched in spirituality rooted in New Age practices, or perhaps you are. Or maybe you just have questions about which beliefs are from God and truly in line with Church teaching and which ones are not. For example, is it acceptable to visit a psychic or read a horoscope to help figure out the future? Perhaps a friend has suggested Reiki, yoga, or acupuncture for healing a long, debilitating illness, and you, at the end of your rope, are considering them. Can a Christian practice one of the many meditation techniques that are known to increase mental health and sanity, such as Mindfulness, Transcendental Meditation, or Zen? Maybe you have been reading inspirational and spiritual books, such as the *The Secret* or *A Course in Miracles,* to better yourself.

It is entirely praiseworthy to seek peace, healing, self-actualization, and the necessary answers that will lead us to wholeness and fulfillment. After all, God has made us to be at peace and to live joy-filled lives in him. Sometimes, however, we reach for a cure that seems to promise us the world but leads instead to destruction and disillusionment. This is one reason why people fall so easily into the trap of false spirituality, which leads souls astray: They are seeking a quick fix. If we truly seek to follow God, to better ourselves, and to find peace, we must have the necessary knowledge to detect what will help us and what will hurt us. Just because a book, a blog post, or a pamphlet mentions God, it doesn't mean that what it recommends is from him. Often it is not.

How can we know the difference? Thankfully, God has intervened to help us in this matter by bestowing on us some marvelous gifts. The first is his divine Son, Jesus Christ. God loves us so much that he came to earth in the person of Jesus Christ more than 2,000 years ago to teach us the fullness of truth. Thus, truth himself came to earth and walked among us. How spectacular!

The second gift is the Catholic Church. Before ascending into heaven, Christ Our Lord founded the Catholic Church to teach and guard truth until the end of time. He also promised to stay with his Church and to guide her into all truth by the Holy Spirit. The Catholic Church, therefore, possesses the fullness of truth, grace, and salvation and holds all the tools needed for our spiritual growth, drawing from God's revelation and from centuries upon centuries of Tradition.

The third gift is the Bible, which is God's very words, written by inspired authors and given to us by the Catholic Church, who determined by her authority which books were divinely inspired.

If we pay attention to these gifts and use them properly, they will transform us, keep us on the straight and narrow path to heaven, sustain our faith, and help us to find the peace, joy, and satisfaction that the world cannot give. These gifts will help us to reap the bounty of God's great, inexpressible love. The road is not always easy, and it is never a quick fix, but the journey is unquestionably worth it.

So do not be duped by the counterfeit, the quick fix, the promise of ease without sacrifice. Counterfeit spiritual beliefs surround us in our culture, and they emerge in unexpected places. There is no shortage of false spirituality being taught, promoted, and practiced close to you: in your state, in your town, even perhaps in your parish. False spirituality also camouflages itself in many disguises, from self-help manuals and popular holistic practices to angel spiritualities and various forms of healing.

The Devil always mixes lies with truth, and this can make discernment difficult. Sadly, even in our Church, ordinary laypeople, theologians, clergy, and religious brothers and sisters have been duped. Many Catholic retreat houses across the country, which people depend on and trust, have bought into New Age spirituality and bogus practices, leading souls astray, even if with the best intentions.

As one example, I attended an eight-hour retreat at one of the largest Catholic retreat facilities in the country. Many Catholics attended, hoping to grow in their faith. Instead, a priest spent several hours teaching us how to reach divine enlightenment (a Buddhist concept) through the practice of Cabbala (a false Jewish mysticism), Zen (a Buddhist practice), and spiritual yoga (a Hindu practice). Nothing resembling authentic Catholicism was even mentioned. I was dismayed to realize that my fellow retreatants saw no problem with this. They were unequipped to recognize the counterfeit spirituality being peddled to them in place of genuine Catholicism. This is especially troubling because we trust retreat houses and other such institutions to provide us with solid Catholic guidance, not erroneous teachings. How many souls are being led astray in similar situations because they assume a Catholic resource will provide guidance in line with the Church's teachings?

This is why it is critical for Catholics to be trained to spot counterfeits, just like bankers with money. This is true not only in the secular world around us but especially in our places of worship and in the resources in which we put our trust. We must inform ourselves well so we will be able to distinguish truth from error and even to help inform others. That is the purpose of this book. In its pages, you will learn to spot the counterfeits and replace them with the truth that is found only in Christ.

We will explore many questions, including:

- May Catholics practice yoga if it is purely for exercise?
- May Catholics participate in Reiki or acupuncture for healing?
- Can astrology or horoscopes help in trying to predict your future?
- Can the Law of Attraction help you to think more positively?
- Is Centering Prayer authentic Catholic prayer?
- What about Enneagrams, labyrinths, mindfulness, Zen, and countless other practices that are popular today?

This book will arm you with the necessary knowledge to answer these and other questions. It will not only serve to increase your awareness and spiritual discernment but will also be a reference for any concerns or questionable practices you may encounter in the future. You may choose to give a copy of this book to someone who has questions about or is entangled in some problematic spiritual practice.

Finding the ultimate truth about spirituality helps us to avoid confusion or something worse. It enables us to share with others the truth that sets us free. It also enables us to find the peace, joy, and freedom we are looking for in every aspect of our lives. So, let's begin this journey!

CHAPTER 1
WHAT IS TRUTH?

Do you love ice cream? (Who doesn't?) What is your favorite flavor? My favorite is black raspberry. You might argue that vanilla is the best ice cream, and someone else might say that chocolate is the best.

How about movies? What is your favorite movie? My favorite is *The Lord of the Rings*. Someone else's may be *Star Wars*, and still another person's might be *The Sound of Music*. We each hold a different truth. These are known as subjective truths, and these differences of opinion are what make the world go 'round.

Subjective truths are opinions that are influenced by different preferences, circumstances, people, and societies. They may even change from one year to the next. What floats one person's boat might not float another's, and what somebody believes is the best, someone else may deem the worst. To each his own. Subjective truths are not absolute because they vary.

Objective truth, on the other hand, is absolute. Two plus two equals four. A triangle has three sides. George Washington was a man. Gravity is a force that causes things to fall toward earth. These truths do not change, even if a person disagrees with them. A wise guy may claim that two plus two equals five, and may even believe it, but his opinion on this matter carries no weight and does not alter the objective truth that two plus two equals four. Likewise, someone may disagree with what science tells us about gravity, but she would be unwise to test her theory by stepping off the top of a building. When something is true, that truth does not and cannot change. We can choose not to accept it, but that does not make it any less true.

It is the same in our spiritual lives. Some people claim that we cannot know truth. Others assert their subjective truths as objective reality. The question is: How can we know the truth? When we investigate this question, we remember that Jesus came to teach us the fullness of truth. In other words, all truth comes from God. We can know the truth precisely because Jesus Christ, the eternal Son of God and second Person of the Trinity, came to earth to deliver it to us. Jesus made the bold claim: "I am the way, and the truth, and the life; no one comes to the Father, but by me" (Jn 14:6).

There have been many other religious leaders and gurus in history, to be sure, but there were none like Jesus. Christ not only made bold claims about being the Most High God; he also worked countless miracles, cast out demons, forgave sins, and rose from the dead to prove that everything he said was true. He made radical claims, and he backed them up with great power and authority. Many religious leaders have claimed to possess *some* truth, but Jesus claimed to bring the *fullness* of truth and even to be truth itself. Therefore, Jesus alone is objective, absolute truth.

Of course, this is not meant to disrespect or insult any other religion or religious leader. Every religion contains aspects of truth, some more than others. No other religious leader, however, can compare with Jesus Christ — his teachings, his miracles, or his legacy. No other religious leader in history opened the eyes of the blind, made the mute speak or the lame walk, or raised the dead. Consequently, no other religion or spiritual leader in history can contradict, correct, add to, fix, or attempt to challenge anything Jesus commanded or taught.

This includes what Jesus delivered to us through his Church, the Catholic Church, and what we read in the Bible, the inspired word of God. "It must be firmly believed that Jesus Christ is the mediator, the fulfillment and the completeness of revelation. It is therefore contrary to the Catholic Faith to maintain that revelation in Jesus Christ (or the revelation of Jesus Christ) is limited, incomplete, lacking or imperfect. ... The historical revelation of Jesus Christ offers everything necessary for man's salvation and has no need of completion by other religions."[1]

The *Catechism of the Catholic Church* states that other religions, including Eastern spiritual traditions, often do have a "ray" of truth (2104). Yet they are not on a par with Christianity. Jesus Christ alone is the fullness of salvation. Moreover, Jesus sent his Holy Spirit to guide the Church into all truth (Jn 16:13). Thus, the Church is the pillar and foundation of truth (1 Tm 3:15), and Jesus promised to be with his Church until the end of time (Mt 28:20).

These truths have been handed on for more than 2,000 years through the Scriptures and the Church, and we can still know them today. Thus, when it comes to discerning authentic Catholic spirituality from the counterfeit, anything that is contrary to Jesus and his word cannot be truth and therefore is not from heaven. The Bible reminds us that the Devil can transform himself into an "angel of light" in order to deceive people (2 Cor 11:14). It also calls Satan the "father of lies" and a "murderer from the beginning" (Jn 8:44). The goal of the evil one is to distort the truth of Jesus Christ, supplant it with a counterfeit, and lead people astray.

Make no mistake: There are countless counterfeits in the world today. This is why Scripture warns us: "But even if we, or an angel from heaven, should preach to you a gospel contrary to that which we have preached to you, let him be accursed. As we have said before, so now I say again, if anyone is preaching to you a gospel contrary to that which you received, let him be accursed" (Gal 1:8–9). Hence, if someone claims to have seen an angel, to have had a spiritual encounter, to have discovered some secret knowledge, or anything similar that contradicts Jesus, the Bible, or his Church, we can be certain that he or she is mistaken. It's that simple.

Recall that Jesus himself warned against false prophets who would arise and preach a different message from his. Others would claim to speak on his behalf or even claim to be him. He warned his followers and us, "Take heed that no one leads you astray. For many will come in my name saying, 'I am the Christ,' and they will lead many astray" (Mt 24:4–5). He goes on, "If any one says to you, 'Behold, here is the Christ!' or 'There he is!' do not believe it. For false Christs and false prophets will arise and show many great signs and wonders. … Behold, I have told you beforehand" (Mt 24:23–25).

Those who practice and promote counterfeit spiritualities often remove what Christ taught and replace it with more subjective beliefs. We must be on guard against this. For example, whereas the true Jesus Christ made it clear that the path to heaven is narrow and difficult, the counterfeit Jesus teaches lessons that demand little or nothing. Likewise, people might claim to be spiritual, not religious, making themselves the authority. Similarly, the counterfeit Jesus allows people to pray at home instead of attending Mass on Sundays or to follow their consciences even when their consciences lead them to go against the Bible or the Church. According to the counterfeit Jesus, it is better to live and let live than to enforce rules and teach the Church's doctrines.

We must be cautious of the Jesus whose only command is to practice a subjective, feelings-based love. This is not the true, self-sacrificial charity that Christ requires, but rather a vague feeling of benevolence toward creation that seeks to supersede God's commandments and teachings. In other words, counterfeit spiritualities decide for themselves what "truth" they choose to follow and what they wish to ignore.

Thankfully, Jesus is honest and clear about the truth and what is needed for salvation. We do not need to guess at it or attempt to figure it out. So, as we begin to look at counterfeit spiritualities and teachings, remember that Jesus has warned us that the journey may be difficult, but it leads to everlasting life. Having the truth of Jesus Christ is like having a road map that leads to heaven. Throw the map away or ignore it, and it will be impossible to arrive at the destination. Follow Jesus and his truth, and your soul will be kept safe on the road to eternity. Anyone who promises to lead you by an easier or faster path than that which Christ has mapped out is a counterfeit.

In the chapters that follow, we will examine some of the many counterfeit beliefs and teachings that pervade our society and our Church and that honest Christians become entangled in. By learning to spot the fakes, you will safeguard your soul and develop the proficiency to help save the souls of others. We will begin by examining some of the more common beliefs and practices that Christians encounter today.

CHAPTER 2
THE NEW AGE PROBLEM

According to astrology, every 2,165 years there is a new age. Astrology teaches that the Age of Pisces (the age of Jesus and Christianity) has passed away, and the "New Age" (the Age of Aquarius) has dawned on us. Whereas the old age had to do with earthly religion, this New Age symbolizes a time of spiritual knowledge and enlightenment, a spiritual awakening. These New Age beliefs have become the bedrock of many movements and popular practices in our country. They claim to be carrying us forward, yet in reality they are a big step backward. In their attempt to move beyond Jesus Christ and his Church, they are leading us back into paganism.

Throughout history, there have been erroneous religions and philosophies. This is the reason Jesus Christ came, to enlighten us. For example, the New Age movement proposes a counterfeit Jesus. Whereas the real Jesus taught that there is only one truth, New Age spirituality blends many non-Christian religions and philosophies that Christ came to bring light to. Whereas the goal of Christianity is to be with Christ in heaven, the goal of the New Age is to provide spiritual knowledge (gnosis) to help people find their own divinity, as will be seen in the pages ahead. Whereas Christians follow Jesus and believe that only his death on the cross can save us, the New Age movement proposes that we can save ourselves through various beliefs and techniques.

According to the false New Age claims, successful spiritual

awakening is accomplished by achieving divine enlightenment, which even Jesus needed to find. Christianity teaches the truth that Jesus is the Son of God, but New Agers make a distinction between the *man* Jesus, who lived over 2,000 years ago, and a perfect divine state known as "the Christ." According to this New Age theory, the man Jesus lived out this Christ state perfectly and set an example for the world in reaching enlightenment. New Age theory teaches that we are called to follow his example, to become Christ, and to achieve the same perfection that he did.

New Age spirituality contains some truth, which is why it can be misleading, but it is also full of many flagrant errors. The goal of those who practice this spirituality is to attain spiritual wholeness and freedom, which is a noble goal. Yet the teachings of this movement turn Jesus into just one avatar among many whom we can follow to achieve enlightenment and find salvation. These false spiritual teachings are built on Hindu and Buddhist philosophies that have an entirely different concept of God, or do not accept the existence of God at all. As we will see, the Christian God and the New Age version of God are very different. This is particularly important for us to understand, as many spiritual beliefs, practices, popular books and magazines, and television shows are based on the false New Age version of "God."

Monism: Everything Is One

The first New Age principle is known as *monism*, or universal oneness. Monism is a Hindu concept that teaches a oneness with everything in the universe. Everything is one and the same without difference or distinction. In other words, there is no difference between people, trees, planets, cars, dogs, milkshakes, or anything else in the universe. Thus, if you ask how many things exist, the answer is: one, and everything is part of that one.

According to monism, the seeming differences and distinctions around us do not actually exist but are illusions that our minds create. To see reality, one must have a complete spiritual awakening, an enlightenment moment. Although it might sound a bit strange and esoteric, this belief of monism forms the foundation of many popular practices, including Reiki, yoga, the Law of Attraction, Zen, the Enneagram, Transcendental Meditation, acupuncture, Qigong, and Feng Shui.

Some of the most popular spiritual books that advocate monism have lined the best-seller racks in bookstores for decades. For example, *The Secret*, by Rhonda Byrne, states, "We are One. We are all connected, and we are all part of the One Energy Field, or the Supreme Mind, or the One Consciousness, or the One Creative Source. Call it whatever you want, but we are all One."[1]

Eckhart Tolle, author of several spiritual best-sellers, also teaches: "The body that you can see and touch is only a thin illusory veil. ... It is this screen of thought that creates this illusion of separateness, the illusion that there is you *and* a totally separate 'other.' You then forget the essential fact that underneath the level of physical appearances and separate forms, you are one with all that is."[2]

This philosophy teaches that whatever humans observe with their physical eyes is only a thin veneer compared with reality — that is to say, the higher spiritual reality. Everything we observe around us is only an illusion or a dream state. Our spirits alone are able to grasp the true reality, so we must bypass our physical senses to achieve this. Thus, our duty is to push our consciousness forward through spiritual knowledge and liberation of the senses. Only then can we arrive at an enlightened spiritual consciousness that will give us true wisdom.

In short, monism posits that everything is one: you, I, our pets, this book, our planet. There is no distinction among us, and we must realize that everything is one and the same thing, all coming from, and part of, the same divine Source. This is connected to pantheism.

Pantheism: Everything Is Divine

The next principle, known as *pantheism*, states that we are all God. In this worldview, God is not a personal being, as Christianity teaches. Rather, what we call "God" is more of a cosmic universal energy that makes up everything in the universe and that every created thing is a part of. New Agers claim that since everything in the universe is made up of energy, and since all energy proceeds from a higher Source (God, or "the Universe"), then all of creation, including humans, is part of God and his very essence. Therefore, New Age beliefs state that all human beings are divine like God.

Some term this "divinization"* or "Ultimate Reality." Hindus call it "Brahman," and different New Agers call it "God-consciousness," "Christ-consciousness," "God-realization," "God-essence," or the "true Self."[3] Whatever term is employed, the underlying meaning is the same: humans are divine.

The absolute oneness of everything includes an absolute oneness with God. *The Secret* teaches this unambiguously: "You are God in a physical body. You are Spirit in the flesh. You are eternal life expressing itself as You. You are all power. You are all wisdom. You are all intelligence. You are perfection."[4] It is troubling to note that this kind of philosophy is promoted by Oprah and other popular celebrities who endorse the book.

Similarly, internationally acclaimed lecturer and best-selling

---

* Christianity speaks of divinization, but not in the counterfeit sense we are discussing. A false understanding of this term is that we become one with God in the sense that we are part of him, an extension of his being, or that we merge with or melt into him. A true and proper Christian understanding of this, however, consists in the understanding that God communicates his divine life to us through grace and the Holy Spirit. We then become more and more *like* God, but the important distinction is that we will never *be* God. This is what many of the early Christians meant when they said God took on our human nature, so we could share in his divine nature. This is confirmed in paragraph 460 of the *Catechism of the Catholic Church*. Likewise, the Church specifically says in the document *Jesus Christ, the Bearer of the Water of Life*, "It is necessary in the first place to bear in mind that man is essentially a creature, and remains such for eternity, so that an absorbing of the human self into the divine self is never possible, not even in the highest states of grace." In other words, we will become "partakers" in God's divine nature through grace, but we will never be God or be divine, as he is.

author Marianne Williamson teaches both monism and pantheism: "We pray to be *reminded* of who we really are so our thoughts and behaviors no longer reflect a dissociation from our divine self. ... In our oneness with others lies our oneness with God, and removing those walls is His work in us and in the world. God's one begotten son is who we are."[5] Notice Williamson asserts that God's only-begotten son is not Jesus, as Christians teach, but all of us as one being.

Eckhart Tolle also teaches that we must achieve this divine state, just as Jesus did: "[Jesus] was a man who lived two thousand years ago and realized divine presence, his true nature. ... Thus, the man Jesus became Christ, a vehicle for pure consciousness." Tolle continues, "Christ is your God-essence. The only difference between Christ and presence is that Christ refers to your indwelling divinity regardless of whether you are conscious of it or not, whereas presence means your awakened divinity or God-essence."[6]

One of the best-selling spiritual books of all time, *A Course in Miracles*, teaches that we have a "true Self" and a "false self." The false self is our earthly body, which lives in illusion, and our true Self (capital *S* to show divinity) is divine and one with God.[7] *A Course in Miracles* teaches that we are sinless and as perfect as God: "The false self you made, evil and full of sin is meaningless. Your sinlessness is guaranteed by God. ... You are one Self, the holy Son of God, united with your brothers in that Self, united with your Father in His Will. ... This is your Self, the Son of God Himself, as sinless as its Creator."[8]

Best-selling author and motivational speaker Dr. Wayne Dyer wrote, "You are eternally light and divine no matter what you have done or failed to do." He also says, "We are all extensions of the same God, manifested in a physical form with specific identifiable attributes. ... In truth, none of us are separate from God. None of us are separate from each other."[9]

Dozens and dozens of popular books could be quoted at length to demonstrate that these monistic and pantheistic teachings dominate our culture and thought. These books are promoted as self-help manuals and motivational works, so it is easy to be swept away by the positive ideas while missing the incredibly problematic teachings that contradict the very core truths of our faith. Unfortunately, even some Catholics have been duped by pantheistic ideas. For example, Father Thomas Keating writes, "God and our true Self are not separate. Though we are not God, God and our true Self are the same thing."[10] (Note that the "S" in "Self" is capitalized to show divinity.)

We must realize that these teachings contain kernels of truth, but in reality, they are erroneous and spiritually spurious. For example, Christians believe that we are called to be in union *with* God and will be *like* God someday in heaven, but we will never *be* God. Also, Christ calls us to live in unity with others and with creation, but we will always remain our own distinct, individual persons; we will not meld with the "universal consciousness." This twisting of truth and blending of half-truths make detecting the reality more difficult, which is why many are led astray.

In the next section, we will look a little more deeply at the problems of New Age teaching and what dangerous conclusions it leads to.

CHAPTER 3

THE LAW OF
ATTRACTION

In the last chapter, we discussed New Age spirituality and some of its core beliefs, which pull from multiple religions, including even the occult (see the next chapter). We briefly examined the foundational principles of monism (everything is one) and pantheism (everything is divine). In this chapter, we will follow these beliefs to their logical conclusions and show why they lead to a spiritually dangerous worldview void of the true God.

New Age spirituality teaches that there is no Devil, no evil, and no right and wrong. Why? Well, if we accept the nondualistic principle that everything is one, and everything is God (who is all-good), then evil and sin are illusions and do not exist. Consequently, the Devil is a lie, hell is not real, and what Jesus taught us was mistaken. Moreover, Christian theology has been wrong for more than 2,000 years.

Popular spiritual philosophies of today teach precisely this. Neale Donald Walsch is just one of many influential spiritual teachers who propagate this message. In his immensely popular, best-selling series, *Conversations with God*, Walsch states, "Hitler went to heaven for the following reasons: there is no hell, so there is no place else for him to go. His actions were what you would call mistakes. ... The mistakes Hitler made did no harm or damage to those whose deaths he caused."[1] Further down on the same page, he states, "Everything occurring in the universe is occurring perfectly. God hasn't made a mistake in a long time."

This worldview, which removes all consequences for actions, is not only seriously flawed; it is also dangerous. According to this mindset, what is to stop future Hitlers from performing similar atrocities? If evil does not exist, and there are no consequences for our actions, then people can act in any way they like without concern. As Christians, we recognize that this belief contradicts Jesus, who made it crystal clear that evil is real and that both sin and hell exist (see, for example, Matthew 13:41–43; 25:31–46; Mark 9:45–48, among many other Scripture verses). So we can know with certainty that any other teaching about hell is a counterfeit. This is the very reason Jesus died on the cross, to ransom us from sin. If evil does not exist, then Jesus died for nothing, and his death was in vain.

Another belief that follows from monism and pantheism is the Law of Attraction, also known as the Human Potential Movement. According to this belief, since we are divine, and part of God, our minds are all-powerful like his, and they will obey us and do exactly as we think. So, if we think positively, we will attract good things to ourselves, such as money, power, fame, and love. In contrast, thinking negatively will attract negative circumstances into our lives — car accidents, sexual abuse, pain, depression, disease, and poverty, to name a few. Some of the most influential spiritual books and motivational speakers today promote this line of thinking. It is found in seminars, retreat houses, schools, and even businesses where speakers are hired to teach these principles to employees.

In short, the Law of Attraction states that human beings attract everything to themselves, good or bad, simply by how they think. This happens through positive or negative vibrations emanating from our minds into the universe. *The Secret* explains, "Everything that is coming into your life you are attracting to your life. And it's attracted to you by virtue of the images you're holding in your mind. ... The law of attraction says that like attracts like, and so as you think a thought, you are attracting like thoughts to you."[2]

Of course, this principle does contain an element of truth. It is certainly true that thinking more positively in life is beneficial, both mentally and spiritually. Doing so helps us to achieve our goals more readily, to feel better about ourselves, and even to be more successful. Having a more positive mindset also enables us to have more self-confidence — say, to ask someone out on a date — and even to have a better relationship with God, since a positive mindset makes us more open to his action in our lives.

The converse is also true. If we struggle with low self-esteem and often think negatively about ourselves and the world around us, we will not be as confident on a job interview, when engaging in relationships, or even when trying to grow in our walk with God. Positivity does not accomplish these things for us, but it can improve our disposition, which will allow us to attempt things more frequently, to grow more eagerly, and most likely, to succeed more often. Scripture tells us that we must allow God to renew and transform our minds (see Rom 12:2). So, if you struggle with negativity and are looking to be transformed mentally and spiritually, this desire is good and worthwhile, and God can bring that healing about in your life. But this is very different from the "positive thinking" encouraged by the Law of Attraction.

The Law of Attraction takes a basic truth (that it is good for us to think positively) and twists it into a deceptive lie. Masquerading as a motivational teaching, this principle goes too far, because it posits that the human mind holds infinite power to accomplish anything it desires. The Law of Attraction assumes that the human mind is divine and can create its own reality. At its core, the Law of Attraction reverses the Christian prayer "thy will be done" into "my will be done."

Was not this the first temptation by the Devil? He promised Adam and Eve that they would be like God by eating from the fruit of the tree (Gn 3:5). In the same way, the Law of Attraction teaches that we are gods and the creators of all. According to *The*

Secret, "Like Aladdin's Genie, the law of attraction grants your every command. ... We are the creators, not only of our personal destiny, but ultimately, we are creators of ultimate destiny. We are the creators of the Universe."[3] Can you see how the Law of Attraction replaces God with self? It states that we, not God, are fully in control of what happens to us. Thus, the takeaway is that we do not have to rely on God or trust in his plan.

Beyond its pantheistic origins and belief, the Law of Attraction has other problems. Since it requires that people think positively and assumes that positive thinking attracts good things into our lives while negative thinking attracts bad, this law often leads proponents to ignore the problems of the world in favor of "positivity." Since "like attracts like," followers of this thinking intentionally avoid negative circumstances or suffering individuals for fear of attracting that suffering into their own lives. Many who adhere to the Law of Attraction will even blame victims for the sufferings they experience. According to this mindset, tragedies such as getting sick, experiencing a natural disaster, or suffering sexual abuse could have been averted if the victims had thought more positively more often.

This is spelled out clearly in *The Secret*: "Disease is held in the body by thought, by observation of the illness, and by the attention given to the illness. If you are feeling a little unwell, do not talk about it — unless you want more of it. If you listen to people talk about their illness, you add energy to their illness."[4]

Walsch's *Conversations with God* also addresses this: "Events are occurrences in time and space which you produce out of choice. ... Some events you produce willfully, and some events you draw to you — more or less unconsciously. Some events — major natural disasters are among those you toss into this category — are written off to 'fate.' Yet even fate can be an acronym for 'from all thoughts everywhere.' In other words, the consciousness of the planet."[5] In other words, according to the Law of Attraction, natural disasters are the result of negative thinking on a massive scale.

In a particularly jarring example, the book *The Jesus Path* teaches that people who are raped have only themselves to blame. They brought this tragedy upon themselves as a result of their own negative thoughts. Worse, this book goes on to claim that this teaching comes straight from Jesus.[6] This worldview is incredibly dangerous, and not at all rooted in the true teachings of Jesus Christ.

Sharon Lee Giganti is a convert to the Catholic Church, a professional speaker, and a former New Age practitioner. Before her conversion, she subscribed to the Law of Attraction and lived it out as fully as possible. She reveals her own heartbreaking story and the terrible repercussions of this line of thinking. She openly admits that in her life, she ignored loved ones around her who were desperately in need of her help because she refused to be burdened by their negativity. She now believes that her adherence to the Law of Attraction contributed to the suffering, imprisonment, and even dying of people she knew.[7]

The Christian Response

Jesus healed people, helped people, forgave sins, raised people from the dead, and paid particular attention to the poor and those who were suffering in this world. He instructed his followers to do the same, commanding us to pick up our crosses and to serve our brothers and sisters in order to be his disciples (Mt 25:31–46; Jas 2:14–18). Moreover, the God-man himself, Jesus Christ, suffered out of love for the world, dying on the cross. Did Jesus attract that suffering to himself? Did he do something wrong or think too negatively? Of course not; Jesus conquered and redeemed suffering, thus teaching us that we can find peace in any circumstances, no matter what challenges we face.

Thinking positively and working to better our lives are very good things. As Christians, however, we should always be subject to God, his holy will, and what he wants for us in our lives. We can choose our jobs, make life decisions, plan, and work toward achieving goals, but ultimately, we are not God and never will be. Everything is in God's control and in his powerful hands. He may well choose to lead us in a direction different from the one we had planned. In this, we must be open and prayerfully discerning. Only God is God, and only he has the infinite wisdom and knowledge to understand all things.

The truth is that nobody can do anything without God's grace (Jn 15:5), and no one is capable, therefore, of creating his or her own reality. We cannot exist, breathe, walk, obtain salvation, or anything else without Our Lord working his grace and power in our lives. Thus, for Christians, life is a journey and a relationship with Our Lord, not something we go at alone. We must pray often and seek God's will in all things.

For Christians, thinking positively is not about controlling our destiny or changing our world or our situations. It is about changing the way we react to the things that happen in our lives. Although we do not accept the Law of Attraction, we do believe that becoming stronger both mentally and spiritually is important for our lives, and it improves our relationship with God. We should certainly work to improve ourselves. This may include prayer, counseling, spiritual direction, and reading *good* self-help books.

In addition, we must work to be a light to the world. As faithful followers of the Lord Jesus, we must strive to be the antidote to the world's suffering through intentional love, mercy, and self-sacrifice. Christ taught that serving others is the same as serving him. The easy and comfortable path that seeks to avoid all pain and suffering is not the path to heaven! Christ said we must pick up our cross and follow him. Only then we will receive a full reward in heaven and all the glory that comes with it.

CHAPTER 4
ASTROLOGY AND THE OCCULT

One winter, my best friend and I were pretending to be superheroes with other kids in the neighborhood. At top speed, we ran around the perimeter of a house as fast as our little ten-year-old legs would carry us. Believing we had super speed, nothing could possibly stop us. Then it happened!

Around the corner was a German shepherd coddling his food. Completely oblivious, I bounded too close to this huge dog and his dish. Even though he was tied to a running wire, he immediately lunged at me, catching the back of my coat with his claws and dragging me backward to the ground. The next minute will forever be etched into my memory. I still remember the vivid sounds of deep snarls and loud growls all around me and the sound of my coat being torn apart as the dog sank his teeth and claws into me again and again.

By some miracle, I managed to pull myself out of the dog's mighty grasp. Once more the dog lunged at me, but this time I was safely out of his reach. In terror, I ran across the street to my mother, looking back only once to see if the dog was chasing me. If not for my oversized, puffy coat, which encompassed me like a giant marshmallow, I might have suffered severe injuries or even death. It was a blessing that I walked away unscathed that day!

Saint Padre Pio once described the Devil as a rabid dog tied to a chain. As long as we do not place ourselves within his striking distance, he cannot harm us. Unfortunately, by participating in occult or New Age practices, many people unknowingly put themselves in the Devil's reach. These practices open doorways to evil that should never be opened. It can all happen quickly, too, without one's even being aware that the most ferocious beast of all lurks unseen, waiting.

What Is the Occult?

The term "occult" pertains to knowledge of secret, paranormal, or supernatural powers, which include Wicca and witchcraft, magic, Ouija boards, fortune-telling, séances, divination, astrology, tarot cards, crystals, and any other spiritual practices that attempt to foresee the future, contact the dead, or take part in paranormal activity not from God. These things can be harmful to our lives and dangerous to our immortal souls.

Why do people fall into the occult? For some, it is simply out of curiosity. Others have fallen away from their Faith and are seeking to fill a spiritual void in their lives. Still others have had turmoil or a catastrophe strike. As a result, they may begin to look for some wisdom, guidance, or quick fixes for their problems. Consequently, they may consult horoscopes or palm readers, or even visit psychics with the hope of finding the enlightenment they desire. Others may take part in séances, consult mediums, or use Ouija boards to try to communicate with loved ones who have departed this world.

Whatever the reason, too many people casually approach these occult practices as if they are harmless. Perhaps you took part in something like this and "nothing happened." You are blessed. You were lucky, as I was with the German shepherd. If I had remained on the ground and not struggled with all my might to escape, however, I could have been severely injured or worse. The same holds true with practices of the occult, because the outcome is dangerous and even deadly for our souls.

Father Gabriele Amorth was the chief exorcist of Rome and

a leading authority on exorcism and spiritual warfare. He helped tens of thousands of people who were harassed by Satan physically, mentally, and spiritually, or who were fully possessed. He had dealings with the evil one each day. He manifestly warned about the dangers of participating even innocently in the occult.

In his book *An Exorcist: More Stories*, Father Amorth states, "There are many ways to contract a bond with the Devil through carelessness. For instance, when we visit magicians or card readers committed to magic practices we forge a bond with them and, through them, with the demon. The same is true when we befriend practitioners of necromancy or spiritualists' séances. We also risk developing ties with the demon by practicing the occult, basing our actions on the careless use of the pendulum or the horoscope, and so on. All these bonds must be severed."[1]

All of this applies even more to Christians. After all, the First Commandment states, "You shall have no other gods before me" (Ex 20:3). In other words, God must be number one in our lives. He is the eternal, all-knowing, all-powerful Creator of all things. He alone sees the past, present, and future, every moment in perfect clarity. Thus, to trust in anything other than God would be inferior, deceiving, and insulting to his infinite majesty.

The great news is that God is not some faraway being beyond the galaxies, or some impersonal force that is part of the universe. Rather, he is a God of love, who is incredibly invested in our lives and is present here with us. He is aware of the difficulties, sufferings, and trials we face, and he may even allow them temporarily in order to draw us closer to himself.

We must realize that God wholly desires to love us, lead us, provide for us, have a deeply personal and abiding relationship with us, and most of all, bring us to heaven. He perpetually works for our good, even when we think we know better. Therefore, by putting any trust in horoscopes, psychics, mediums, or anything else that attempts to foretell the future, we push God to the side. Choosing to trust in anything other than God conveys the message "I don't need you," or worse, "I don't *trust* you. I will figure everything out without you."

Acting on this attitude not only breaks the First Commandment; it also breaks God's heart. God is able to help you, and only he understands what you truly need, far more than anyone (or anything) else. He is absolutely capable of revealing the future to anyone at any time. Our good Lord also knows what is best for us, what will lead us into danger, and what will lead to our happiness and salvation. But even if he does not choose to reveal the future to us, or if he chooses to reveal it only a little at a time, he still expects us to trust him and his divine plan for our lives. God knows all things, so it is not right to run off after false gods or mediums to divine the future for ourselves.

Sacred Scripture often warns us against turning to false idols. The Bible states, "There shall not be found among you any one ... who practices divination, a soothsayer, or an augur, or a sorcerer, or a charmer, or a medium, or a wizard, or a necromancer. For whoever does these things is an abomination to the Lord, and because of these abominable practices the Lord your God is driving them out before you" (Dt 18:10–12).[2]

The *Catechism of the Catholic Church* also warns us against these idols: "All forms of *divination* are to be rejected: recourse to Satan or demons, conjuring up the dead or other practices falsely supposed to 'unveil' the future. Consulting horoscopes, astrology, palm reading, interpretation of omens and lots, the phenomenon of clairvoyance, and recourse to mediums, all conceal a desire for power over time, history, and in the last analysis, other human beings, as well as a wish to conceal hidden powers. They contradict the honor, respect, and loving fear that we owe to God alone" (2116).

Let us now look at some of the popular and seemingly innocent occult practices that harm our relationship with God, lead us astray, and damage our eternal souls.

Astrology

People often ask, "What's your sign?" When they ask me, I immediately make the Sign of the Cross and respond, "Jesus," with a big grin on my face. In astrology, one's "sign" means something different. It refers to the zodiac constellation you were born under, and it supposedly reveals a lot about who you are and will be as a person. This can be summed up in the astrological principle "as above, so below,"[3] meaning that whatever takes place in the heavens will affect what happens to us here on earth.

Astrology claims to provide a way for people to discover information about themselves, their temperaments, their life's purpose, and more. To accomplish this, an astrologer has to know where the planets were at the moment of a person's birth and what sign he or she was born under. Why should that matter, and why is it necessary?

It matters because each sign offers a different meaning and purpose that supposedly tells who a person is as an individual. This makes sense when we understand that astrology began as an ancient pagan practice, in which the sun, the moon, the stars, and the planets were all believed to have an influence over a person's life. According to astrology, each sign of the zodiac is ruled by a different planet. Each planet is believed to be ruled (or even inhabited) by a different god. For example, the planet Mars is inhabited by Mars, the god of war; Venus, the goddess of love, is believed to occupy the planet Venus; and so on. Thus, every planet is ruled by a different god, and each of these gods possesses different temperaments and characteristics, which they pass on to persons born under their sign. For example, a person born in March under Mars (the god of war) will tend to be angry and aggressive, whereas a person born in a month of Venus (the goddess of love) will naturally lead a more gentle, altruistic life. The constellation Aries is also ruled by Mars. Therefore, people born under the sign of Aries will be assertive, ambitious, and even aggressive.

The goal of astrology is to foretell the future, to divine who we are as persons, and to discover our life's purpose and fate. How does this work?

The ecliptic is an area of the sky that the sun appears to move through over a period of a year. As it moves, it appears to pass through thirteen constellations, also known as zodiac constellations. The zodiac of constellations is divided by astrologers into twelve equal sections (though they are not equal in reality) of thirty degrees each. It is said that the sun spends about thirty days in each sign, or constellation, of the zodiac. Different planets rule over a particular zodiac sign, and in some cases, more than one. So, it is the job of the astrologer to locate the planets on a given day in relation to the zodiac constellations. A trained astrologer uses a chart, which is basically a map of the sky as a full circle with the earth at the center. This map depicts where the sun, the moon, and the planets in our solar system are in relation to the earth at any chosen moment.

Why is astrology a problem for us as Christians? Aside from its pagan roots, if the stars and zodiacs determine our personality and our inevitable fates, then God does not have any influence in our lives or decision-making, and neither do we. It should be fairly easy for a Christian to discern a host of problems in this line of thinking.

Some people confuse astrology with astronomy, which is the authentic study of the stars and planets from a purely scientific perspective. Astrology is more of a pseudoscience that studies the stars and planets with a primary focus on the "spiritual" facets. Not surprisingly, astrology does not match up to the scientific data of astronomy. Astrology attempts to reveal who a person is based upon signs revealed by the zodiac. Astrology purports that the sun remains in each sign for about thirty days, or one month, and it takes about one year for the sun to pass through each of the twelve signs. Every month (roughly) possesses a different sign. What ancient astrologers did not know, and what modern astrologers will not usually reveal, is that the zodiac signs have shifted over time due to the gravitational pull of the moon. Thus, the astrological calendar no longer corresponds with the reality of the skies and scientific data. In other words, from a purely scientific perspective, astrology is using inaccurate information, and therefore, the zodiac signs are off and incorrect.

Astronomer Parke Kunkle says, "Since the Babylonian zodiac periods were established millennia ago, the moon's gravitational pull has made the earth 'wobble' around its axis in a process called precession. That has created a one-month bump in the stars' alignment, meaning that 'when [astrologers] say that the sun is in Pisces, it's really not in Pisces.'"[4]

Scientists who study the sun, the planets, and the constellations for a living and use authentic scientific data confirm this:

> Unbeknownst to the ancient astrologers, Earth continually wobbles around its axis in a 25,800-year cycle. This wobble — called precession — is caused by the gravitational attraction of the moon on Earth's equatorial bulge. Over the past two-and-a-half millennia, this wobble has caused the intersection point between the celestial equator and the ecliptic to move west along the ecliptic by 36 degrees, or almost exactly one-tenth of the way around, to the border of Pisces and Aquarius. This means that the signs have slipped one-tenth — or almost one whole month — of the way around the sky to the west, relative to the stars beyond.[5]

In plain English, the alignment of the stars has shifted over time, throwing off each sign by a period of about thirty days — one whole sign. This means that, even if the stars could predict our personalities and behaviors, *the zodiac month traditionally assigned to a person's birth date is incorrect* and therefore does not carry his or her true reading. Likewise, it does not reflect anything true about a person, allegedly born under a certain sign, or that person's temperament.*

In 2016, NASA updated an article on its children's site, Nasa Space Place, that confirmed the truths of an ever-changing universe. The "news" exploded across the astrological community. As one person frantically stated, "We don't want to be dramatic, but NASA just ruined our lives. For the first time in 3,000 years, they've decided to update the astrological signs. This means that the majority of us are about to experience a total identity crisis."[6] Of course, NASA did not change the zodiac signs, but merely acknowledged the reality of the constellation alignments based on the stars' true positions in the sky.

Many scientific studies have confirmed that astrology is unscientific: "There's very little peer-reviewed research into astrology, and as the University of California Berkeley's Understanding Science page puts it, 'As reflected by the minimal level of research in the field, [astrologers] rarely try to test their arguments in fair ways. In addition, the astrological community largely ignores evidence that contradicts its ideas.' "[7]

So, astrology is not true science. At best, it's a pseudoscience. Many studies have confirmed this and have revealed many of the errors in horoscopes and other astrological practices. For example, one rigorous study revealed that out of 3,000 horoscope predictions, only about 10 percent proved true.[8] Other studies have found that those who read horoscopes for a living cannot recognize their own reading when it is placed in front of them among other readings.[9] Surely, if these people possessed true clairvoyance or an understanding of the zodiac, the trained reader could identify his or her own reading in a heartbeat. Other studies show that when a horoscope is sent to ten astrologers, the reading will be interpreted in ten ways. This also shows how inaccurate these readings are.

---

* In addition, according to both ancient and modern science, there are other constellations that astrologers just ignore. The biggest is Ophiuchus, but there are several others, too.

When people read horoscopes and accept astrology as true, they tend to accept what they are told about themselves and their lives, whether it is true or not. Many times, they take only things that seem to apply to them and ignore the rest. This may lead people to believe that horoscopes are accurate when they are not. This was proven by a French researcher and statistician named Michel Gauquelin, who offered a free astrological reading in a newspaper. More than 150 people responded, and each was sent a free 10-page horoscope. Of the people who responded, 94 percent reported satisfaction with the horoscope reading and claimed it was an accurate portrayal of them, and 90 percent of their family members said the same thing. What they did not know is that everyone received the *same* horoscope reading; the reading was the horoscope of Dr. Marcel Petiot, one of the most notorious mass murderers in all of French history.[10] Gauquelin did many other experiments and tests to prove the validity of astrology, and all came up empty. Many of the tests contradicted each other, and he ended up having a mental breakdown.

These are only a few of the many studies that demonstrate the illegitimacy of astrology and horoscopes. When scrutinized under a scientific analysis, astrological readings are deceitful, or merely subjective at best. Sadly, many innocent people are duped by astrologers, and many of these practitioners walk away with large amounts of money. For example, Sylvia Browne was one of the most acclaimed and sought-after psychics in the world. She was so famous that sometimes police departments asked her to help solve murders.[11] She charged people up to $700 for a twenty-minute session. This took place for decades until Browne was discovered to be a fraud. The *Huffington Post* published a long article exposing her fraudulent practice, providing a list of her failed predictions.[12]

This is par for the course. Many astrologers, tarot card readers, psychics, palm readers, and the like simply take advantage of gullible people, and they make a load of money in the process. Virtually every reader, psychic, and medium is a fraud.[13] Even some psychics themselves have come out and admitted they were scamming people.[14] Some who visit astrologers and other fortune-tellers may object that their reader told them things nobody could have ever known. While it seems legitimate, this is a learned art of manipulation. Don't be fooled!

For a trained reader, it is very easy to produce and reproduce "real" answers for people to hear. Matthew Arnold, a former tarot card reader, unveils how unbelievably simple it is to cheat people while raking in large amounts of money. Before his conversion to Jesus, Arnold perfected the art of ripping people off. He says: "You learn to use the person's name, and flattery; you manipulate the conversation to make them agree with the reading as it progresses. But, most of all, I learned to bombard my clients with conflicting information. Now, they're so busy making connections, that afterwards they're only able to remember what applied to them, and really not only my words, so much as the connections that they had made in their own minds which makes it seem even more accurate."[15] Arnold knew full well that he was taking advantage of people, and he cashed in on it.[16] Many readers and psychics are in the business of fraud. Some, perhaps, believe that they are helping people, but in reality they are not.

> Although most of these businesses are scams, there are some people who are truly clairvoyant or audiovoyant.† Such people are rare, but they do possess a dark, supernatural power that is not from God. People with these abilities are even more dangerous than those who intentionally scam people. Their use of astrology is an occult practice based on paranormal powers, and we should avoid them far more than we do the frauds. Whether practiced by those with real powers or not, all astrology is a form of divination that contradicts God.

---

† That is, seeing and hearing hidden things that humans could never know on their own.

Moira Noonan, a former New Age practitioner, professional psychic, and clairvoyant, had a conversion to Jesus Christ and the Catholic Faith. In her book *Ransomed from Darkness*, she describes knowing firsthand the great dangers involved in her work. She describes the messages given to her that would play over and over again in her head like a record. She also recounts the long hours of demonic deliverance needed from a priest to liberate her from the Devil's grip.

Marcia Montenegro, another former astrologer and clairvoyant who has come back to the Lord Jesus, states, "Being an occult art, astrology is connected to the paranormal powers of the occult. This paranormal effect manifested for me when I would concentrate on a chart in preparation for a reading or during the session with the client: I would feel a distinct energy flowing between the chart and myself." She goes on to reveal that she had "psychic flashes" in which she would hear words and see visions. "As someone who was involved in this and related areas for a number of years, I can attest to the dangers inherent in these practices."[17]

Likewise, exorcist Father Gabriele Amorth warns against these dark gifts. He says, "Particular sensibilities tend to go hand in hand with evil disturbances, for instance, predicting the future; intimate knowledge of the presence of evil forces, or of unusual powers in some individuals; most of all hearing voices and seeing visions."[18]

Ouija Boards, the Occult, and Contacting the Dead

Did you know that the movie *The Exorcist* is based on a true story of possession that occurred in the 1970s? This gripping blockbuster unleashed torrents of scary images that have become engraved in our memories. The big question many people have is how such a young child could become possessed. In the true story, the child became possessed by playing with a Ouija board and contacting a spirit.

People dabble in these practices all the time, assuming that things like Ouija boards are largely harmless. Nothing could be further from the truth. Moira Noonan speaks to the terrifying reality behind these practices: "People often came to our séances in order to contact their loved ones who had passed away. That is not what they saw. The truth is that they called upon demons without knowing it. The demons would play whatever roles they were asked to — relatives, spirit guides, and familiar people."[19]

Father Amorth adds useful information regarding these dangers: "There are no good spirits other than angels; there are no evil spirits other than demons. ... The souls of those who die go immediately to heaven or to hell or to purgatory. The souls of the dead present during séances or the souls of the dead who are present in living bodies to torture them are none other than demons."[20] Later he writes, "It may happen that these spirits — who are always and only demons — will possess some of those who participate in the séance. The Church has always condemned séances and participation in them. We never learn anything useful by consulting Satan."[21]

In the movie *The Exorcist*, the priest cannot cast out the Devil because the evil is too strong. The Devil mocks the priest and laughs in his face as he attempts to free the child from possession. Then, in a rage, the priest jumps on the little girl and shakes her wildly. As the Devil continues to laugh and mock him, the priest yells to the Devil, "Take *me*, take *me*!" And then it happens. The transference takes place, and the priest becomes possessed. He immediately goes crazy and jumps out a second-story window to his death. End of movie. Roll credits.

Many people did not sleep for weeks after seeing *The Exorcist*. That ending is not really what happened, however. That was Hollywood's version. The documentary *In the Grip of Evil* tells the true story. First, it was a boy who was possessed, not a girl. Second, the priest did not become possessed. Rather, he called upon the mighty Archangel Michael, who descended in glorious fashion and entered into the possessed boy. A battle between Michael and the Devil ensued, and a loud booming voice rang through the room: "I am Michael, and you will leave this boy *now!*" At that point, the Devil left the boy, never to return.

God was victorious! He is infinitely stronger than the Devil, who is a mere fallen angel, and Hollywood always portrays him as much stronger than he is. But the Devil is far more powerful than we humans are, and when we place ourselves in his grasp, he has no mercy. This is why the safest path in life is to remain close to our Savior, Jesus Christ, who conquered Satan and all of hell. Throughout Scripture, Christ casts out demons with just a word. In the end, God alone will reign supreme in power, glory, and divine majesty. He desires us to join him in the light, but we must remain faithful and follow him.

Christian Psychics?

There can be no Christian psychics or mediums, as these practices are condemned in the Bible. Certain psychics, such as the famous medium John Edward, purport to be Christian, but their activities are not compatible with Christianity. Matthew Arnold says, "If some so-called gift directly opposes Scripture and the *Catechism*, do you really think that all such gifts are from God? Counterfeit spiritual powers are not gifts. They always carry a price and possibly even the loss of heaven."[22]

This can be particularly confusing because the Holy Spirit gives charismatic gifts that may seem similar to psychic powers. These charisms include prophecy, words of wisdom, and words of knowledge. The Holy Spirit will sometimes reveal to people with these gifts hidden things about others, or he might impart particular words that they need to hear. He does this in order to help, guide, or bring healing to their lives. When I was in college, a man came up to me as I was praying alone. He handed me a letter and said, "God wants you to know this, brother." Then he left.

I read the letter in a curious wonder. It revealed my deepest longings and fears with pinpoint accuracy, yet I had never met this man. This experience also helped me with particular issues I was struggling with at the time and propelled me closer to God. Years later, I would likewise be guided by the Holy Spirit to offer people messages of healing from God.

One day, the Lord put a message on my heart for a particular young lady. When I shared it with her, her eyes widened, her mouth dropped open, and after a moment, she asked, "How did you know that? Nobody knows that, not even my mother! Only my boyfriend knows, and I only recently told him." I shared how God revealed it to me for her good and because God wanted to work in her life and heal her. I share this story to make it clear that Christians can be open to the true gifts of heaven if they follow the promptings of the Holy Spirit and seek to do God's will with all their hearts. These gifts must be used in the right way and for the right reasons, however: they should bring us closer to God and should be used for our good and the good of other people. A good Christian does not make a show of the gifts of God or charge money for them. These gifts bring us closer to Jesus and his Church, whereas a dark power or false counterfeit has the opposite effect.

* * *

No matter how steeped in New Age or occult practices (from dabbling to full practice) someone may be, the path back is always the same: prayer, repentance, and following Jesus with all one's heart. Anyone, at any time, can return to the Lord of heaven and earth — it is never too late. The more we give ourselves over to the light, the less darkness has a hold on us. This goes for all Christians and for anyone who wishes to live for God and avoid evil.

Thankfully, the Church provides us with many aids to stay away from occult practices and the power of and the evil one. The best way to draw close to God is through prayer and the sacraments, especially confession and the Eucharist. Confession is known as the "sacrament of healing." In this powerful sacrament, God's mercy, love, and healing are poured out in abundance on those who repent. Only our Lord can restore the pieces of our lives that are broken, lost, or in need of transformation. Only he can write straight with the crooked lines we make, and only he can give us back our wasted time with new, abundant life. Seek him and stay close to him each day.

There are many other helpful methods for uniting yourself more closely to Jesus and for keeping away from the Devil and the occult. For example, the Rosary is extremely powerful, as is the Saint Michael prayer. Reading the Bible will foster your faith life abundantly. Read the New Testament and the stories of Jesus, and get to know him. Read the lives of the saints. Take time for spiritual reading from solid Catholic books. Spiritual reading will guide you on the straight and narrow path to heaven and help you to understand your faith more deeply. It will also aid you in accepting the events and catastrophes life throws your way and will enlighten you, strengthen you, and give you a deeper sense of meaning and purpose. Unlike false spiritual practices, these devotions will help you to grow closer to God and come to know him on a deeper level, to pray more effectively, and to find the true wisdom you seek.

CHAPTER 5
YOGA

When you hear the word "yoga," what comes to your mind? Perhaps a picture of a woman standing on her head and contorting herself into a human pretzel. Or maybe it's a group of people stretching on exercise mats at the beach. Perhaps you think of deep breathing and centeredness. These are the average conceptions of yoga for most Westerners today.

What is yoga? Are Catholics permitted to practice it? What if a person does it only for exercise and fitness? People hold many opinions on this subject, from those who believe that yoga is perfectly acceptable without any problems to those who claim that all the yoga poses worship false gods and even the Devil. Naturally, evaluating yoga in a logical, rational manner will help us to answer the questions at hand.

The exact origin of yoga remains a mystery, but the first mention of yoga dates back thousands of years.[1] The first use of the word is found in the Hindu scriptures, the *Katha Upanishad*, from around 2,500 years ago.[2] Thus, in order to find suitable answers to our questions, we must travel back in time to observe the history, purpose, and goals of yoga and how those relate to us today.

Let us state at the outset that yoga is *not* a religion. The earliest references to yoga, however, come from alleged revelations of the Hindu gods Shakti, Krishna, and Shiva, which can be found throughout Hindu scriptures.[3] The belief is that the gods gave this practice to men as the vehicle for obtaining freedom from the material world and for reaching divine enlightenment.

So, although it is true that yoga is not in itself a religion, yoga was formed from Hinduism and is deeply intertwined with Hindu spirituality. As one yoga master explains, "Hindu spirituality — complex, multifaceted, and laden with many layers of interpretation — is best exemplified in yoga. Some may argue that yoga is not Hinduism, that it is universal in its application and therefore not a religion. While this is true, we must remember that yoga came out of the womb of Hinduism. Additionally, yoga, which developed in the fire of Hindu spirituality, was shaped by its philosophies and is ensconced in the Hindu way of life."[4]

In other words, for thousands of years, Hindus owned, practiced, and developed yoga. The philosophy and spirituality of this practice are Hindu through and through. In fact, yoga was considered a means of achieving salvation for thousands of years, and it is how Buddha found Nirvana.

The word "yoga" means "union," "to join," or "integrate." Its goal is to unite a person's body, mind, and spirit with the Universe (also known as the "supreme Self" or "collective consciousness"). It is believed that yoga can free a person from the bonds of Karma (discussed more in chapter 9) and integrate him or her into the collective Oneness of all that is (Hindus see this as Brahman; others view it simply as the Universe or Ultimate Reality). This was the philosophy and practice of yoga for thousands of years, long before it ever emerged in the West.

Over the centuries, different styles of yoga have developed, each with the same goal of spiritual perfection and liberation. The famous Hindu scholar and sage Patanjali brought together all of these beliefs and synthesized them into one system. His *Yoga Sutras* are the most important, foundational texts in the history of yoga. His system is known as "Classical Yoga," or "Raja Yoga" (Kingly Yoga), because it is the oldest, most authoritative systematic practice of yoga. It is likened to a tree with eight branches, or limbs. Understanding these limbs will ultimately lead us to the answer to our question regarding yoga. The eight limbs are:

1. *Yama* – avoiding evil and practicing virtue
2. *Niyama* – religious observance and study
3. *Asana* – steady seat or bodily posture
4. *Pranayama* – deep breathing and breath control
5. *Pratyahara* – withdrawal of the senses from the external world
6. *Dharana* – concentration
7. *Dhyana* – meditation
8. *Samadhi* – union with Brahman/the Universe

The first two stages involve intense fasting, study, and spiritual preparation in order to purify oneself from evil and prepare for the spiritual journey ahead. These values of fasting and purity are something that Hinduism and Christianity share in common. The next two branches include the physical aspect, *asana*, along with deep breathing techniques and breath control. The next three stages consist of quiet mindfulness, meditation, and deep concentration, which lead to the final stage of *samadhi*,[5] or divine enlightenment.

Most Westerners believe that yoga is just stretching and strengthening exercises. Bodily posture — *asana* — however, is only one of the eight limbs. Exercising, stretching, or simply performing poses does not mean that one is practicing yoga. Yoga is much more, and the part cannot be considered the whole. One prominent Hindu leader encapsulates this in relation to Christianity:

It is so unfortunate that the word "yoga" has so often been used in place of the word "asana" or "posture" in recent years. We would not call a brick a "house" even though it is part of the construction. Yet, this is often

done with yoga. ... In modern times, the relative position of the postures has been elevated so as to lead
people to believe that the postures or asanas, that the
goal of these, is physical fitness. The whole and the part
have been reversed, terribly misleading and confusing
people about the true nature of authentic yoga. ... In
Christianity, there is a practice called the communion
rite in which consecrated wine and bread are distrib-
uted to people. The wine is said to be symbolic of the
blood of Jesus Christ. The bread is said to be symbolic
of the body of Jesus Christ. People sometimes have wine
with a meal. If a person drinks wine, does that mean he
or she is practicing the Christian right of Communion?
People sometimes have bread with a meal. If a person
eats bread, does that mean she or he is practicing the
Christian rite of Communion? Or, are the people simply
having wine and bread with their meal? It is self-evi-
dent, that merely drinking wine or eating bread are not
in themselves the same as practicing the sacred communion of Christianity.[6*]

As this author rightly points out, for Christians, simply eating
bread and having a glass of wine does not constitute participation in the Lord's Supper (Holy Communion). In the same way,
merely performing postures, stretching, or exercising is not
yoga, which is a very small part of the whole practice. Yoga is a
complete spiritual way of life built on Hindu spirituality. Therefore, it is not appropriate for Christians to practice or even take
part in yoga.

---

[*] Coming from a Hindu perspective, this author does not understand the Catholic
Church's teaching on Holy Communion. Instead, the author is speaking of the Prot-
estant understanding of communion, which sees the Eucharist as a mere symbol. The
Catholic Church teaches that Jesus Christ is present in the Holy Eucharist, Body, Blood,
Soul, and Divinity.

What About Yoga for Exercise?

Many Christians still wonder if the physical aspects of yoga can be separated from the spiritual. Since the exercises themselves do not constitute yoga, the logical question is whether Christians can perform the exercises and stretches if there is no spirituality involved. Let's dive deeper into the physical practice of yoga to answer this and evaluate whether the postures themselves are good, bad, neutral, or compromised.

Throughout history, the fitness and physical postures as we know them today were not part of yoga. Some assert that yoga, as a complete system of health and wellness, has been passed down to us over thousands of years. This is untrue. Today's *asana* postures and exercises, even the *vinyasa* style,† are a very modern development in yoga.

From the beginning of yogic history, all forms and systems of yoga were about attaining spiritual growth and had virtually nothing to do with fitness. Even the physical form of Hatha yoga was primarily a spiritual practice.[7] The main postures that were utilized in yoga were various forms of seated positions used for meditation. So, if the exercises that we know today did not originate with yoga, where did they come from?

The majority of all *asanas* and stretches were borrowed, appropriated, and synthesized from other physical fitness and strengthening regimes. Specifically, they were taken from "primitive gymnastics" and later Danish gymnastics, YMCA fitness programs,[8] calisthenics, Indian wrestling, Western bodybuilding, women's harmonial gymnastics, and more.[9] In other words, the principal postures and stretches that many assume came from yoga did not originate with yoga but derive from Western influence, mostly in Europe and Great Britain, emerging in the mid-1800s to mid-1900s.

---

† *Vinyasa* involves stringing postures together in order to move from one to the next seamlessly, all while practicing breathing.

Let us take a few quick examples. The first is B. H. Ling, who started a system known as Scandinavian gymnastics (or Swedish gymnastics), which focused on moving postures with a mind, body, and soul connection. The goal of these "medical gymnastics" was to provide holistic physical healing and health through the use of postures and deep breathing. Sound familiar? Ling Gymnastics are just one of several fitness forms from the 1800s that would influence yoga and help to create today's yoga. Likewise, in the early 1900s, Danish gymnastics, or Primitive Gymnastics, exploded in popularity. It was so effective that the British army used it to train their soldiers. The system used intensive stretching and rhythmic exercise movements and was intended to help users develop "flexibility and freedom." In the 1920s, both Scandinavian gymnastics and Primitive Gymnastics were the most popular forms of exercise in all of India.[10]

Harmonial Gymnastics was a movement started in the early twentieth century just for women. It consisted of "spiritual stretching," deep breathing, "gymnastic movement and relaxation."[11] While the various men's exercise regimens were based on strength and postures, this women's movement focused on the idea of spiritual gymnastics, flexibility, and wholeness. Yoga as we know it today pulled from all these exercise systems, along with others. The key point here is that all of these exercise systems predated yoga exercise and *asana* as they are practiced today.

Mark Singleton, an authority on this subject, has done research and a full-scale historical analysis on three continents of *asanas* in connection with yoga. In his book *Yoga Body*, he discusses at length the various influences, physical and spiritual, that would later be adapted by "yoga." Singleton states, " 'Yoga' simply did not, until very late in the day, principally signify anything like the *asana*-heavy systems of today, whether in their 'stretch and relax' mode or more aerobic forms. And, conversely, those techniques that we now recognize as 'yoga' were then (i.e., by the 1930s) already a well-established part of Western physical culture — particularly that intended for women — and were not yet associated with yoga in any way." He also adds that yoga used "radical innovation and experimentation. It is the result of adaptation to new discourses of the body that resulted from India's encounter with modernity."[12]

So, almost all of the postures and stretches we know today in yoga are very modern. The majority of ancient *asanas*, with very few exceptions, were variations of the seated lotus position. There was no "Downward Dog," no "Warrior Pose," no "Power Yoga," or anything or the sort. The word *asana* itself means "seat" or "posture," referring to a seated position for the purpose of meditation.

For this reason, a person who merely performs postures or stretches is not practicing yoga. Yoga is a practice that consists of more than physical exercise. Consequently, since these modern-day postures and stretches did not originate with yoga, and they existed long before their incorporation into yoga, the exercises themselves are not problematic for Christians to practice on their own. After all, exercise is not against Christian faith, and there is nothing wrong with stretching and strengthening. For this reason, is it incorrect to claim, as some Christians do, that anyone who performs postures and stretches associated with yoga is worshipping false gods. In fact, most studios do not practice yoga in this way. The takeaway from this is that the exercises themselves are neutral and existed before yoga teachers ever began to incorporate them into spiritual practices.

The problem arises when the exercises are performed in conjunction with spiritual beliefs and adherences. Yoga itself is not exercise. It is a system of spirituality with many beliefs and practices that are incompatible with Christianity. These include: universal energy, chakras, karma, reincarnation, kundalini, chanting, meditation, the third eye, universal Oneness, connection with your Self (considered a divine Self), connection to the Universe, and more. The physical exercises alone may be neutral, but the practice of yoga, which is spiritual, is something no Christian may take part in. If you choose to utilize the exercises alone, that is fine, but realize that you are not practicing yoga.

What about Yoga Classes?

You may wonder if this applies to taking a yoga class at a local studio or online. Although physical postures and stretches are fine, larger problems loom in most yoga classes. The most obvious problems arise with those yoga teachers who view the spiritual aspect of yoga as indispensable. Christians obviously should not attend these classes.

Care should be taken, however, even with yoga instructors who focus more on the fitness aspect. Many studios and online classes accentuate bodily health, physical fitness, and the reduction of stress, yet many teachers unknowingly promote spiritual ideologies or non-Christian beliefs that are inherent in yoga and conflict with Christian beliefs. Certain principles and practices have caught on in the West and are passed down into many local yoga studios, especially through the training that yoga instructors receive. As mentioned above, it is very common to hear or learn about chakras, energy, and breathing techniques, connection to the Universe or the Self, and other ideologies incompatible with Christian beliefs. This occurs whether the instructors consider themselves spiritual or not. From there, they often pass down these teachings in some way, shape, or form to their classes.

For instance, consider deep breathing. Health professionals teach that breathing and breath control have great health benefits in exercise. This obviously poses no problem for a Christian. Yet deep breathing in yoga often carries a different connotation. It derives from a Hindu and Buddhist belief that the breath is not mere breath but energy, or *prana*. According to Eastern religions, this energy (or breath) is a life-force energy that permeates the entire universe and is found within everyone and in everything. Energy or breath is believed to originate with the goddess Shakti, who fills the universe with her energy and manifests that life force in our breath.[13]

B. K. S. Iyengar, the pioneer and foremost authority on modern Hatha yoga, teaches that this focus on our energy in breathing has a neutralizing effect on the mind to prepare it for deep meditative states and eventually connection to the divine cosmic energy.[14] Breath in this view is about not just bodily health but a path to spiritual enlightenment, which is why many yoga classes have the tradition of sitting peacefully so participants can focus on their breath. It comes from this spiritual tradition and is one of the main tenets of yoga.

Hatha yoga, more than other forms, has particularly dangerous views on the subject of energy, as it is viewed in connection with *kundalini*. *Kundalini* energy is said to exist in each person, envisioned as a serpent living in the person and wrapped around the base of his spine. This serpent lies dormant and is meant to be awakened through deep breathing and breath control. As one advances, this energy unravels and begins to climb from the base of his spine up to his head, and from there, one is supposed to have psychic experiences. Yoga teacher Richard Rosen explains, "The idea behind the practice of Hatha Yoga then is to open these centers of consciousness [chakras] by first awakening the dormant spiritual energy (*kundalini*) in the 'root support' (*muladhara*) center at the base of the spine."[15]

Russill Paul is a yoga master who studied as a Catholic monk and attempted to blend Catholicism and Hinduism. He develops this in more detail:

> The word Shakti means "energy"; the great goddess Shakti is the personification of energy, or shakti. In yoga, the manifestation is *prana*, the life force within the breath. ... The Shakti manifests in the human body as a psychospiritual force called kundalini (and the goddess Kundalini is the personification of this force). Normally, kundalini lies dormant; it is envisioned as a serpent coiled at the base of the spine. ... When kundalini awakens inside of you ... It is almost as though something alien enters your being. You feel it in your

bones and your muscles, and it is not just physical; there
is simultaneously an otherworldly quality to it.[16]

Father Gabriele Amorth and other exorcists strongly warn
against participating in yoga, especially in the spiritual aspects,
meditation, and beliefs like *kundalini*. These practices can, and
have, opened people up to demonic spirits.[17] For this reason,
Christians are wise to avoid yoga classes and studios, as they
often contain these deeply problematic elements in some fashion. Even yoga instructors who believe in God or are Christian
do not usually succeed in completely removing the problematic and incompatible teachings associated with Hinduism or the
New Age. In part, this is because they are not informed or cat-
echized enough to do so effectively and do not recognize the
Hindu or New Age influences that have been passed on to them.
So, although they may attempt to lessen the spirituality of their
classes, they often unintentionally keep certain spiritual or philosophical components that Christians should not take part in.

Although it may be tempting to attend classes anyway and
simply ignore the spirituality, it is unwise and unnecessary to
put yourself in that situation. First, you should never needlessly
expose yourself to possible spiritual dangers. Second, as a Christian, you must beware of causing scandal, which is giving a bad
witness of Jesus Christ or the Catholic Faith by one's words or
behavior. This can be a serious sin. For example, if you take part
in yoga classes, others will observe you doing so. They cannot
know which aspects of the class you are simply ignoring or trying to block out. From their perspective, if you sit in meditation,
even if you are thinking about Jesus, you appear to be approv-
ing of a problematic spiritual practice and even taking part in it.
Moreover, people who know that you practice yoga may begin
participating in classes themselves, opening themselves up to all
sorts of spiritual problems.

Where does this leave us? If you would like to do the physical stretches, strengthening, and conditioning in the comfort of

your home, that is fine, as long there is no spirituality involved in any way. If you watch videos or use apps, weed out the ones that have anything harmful or problematic attached to them. Find programs that focus only on the fitness aspect. Furthermore, be careful about the way you describe your exercising. Beware of telling people that you "do yoga," because, in fact, you are not doing yoga; you are doing stretching and strengthening exercises to become more physically fit.

It is helpful to know that there are exercise alternatives that provide a similar or equivalent kind of workout. Pilates, for example, is a good alternative focused more on strengthening. Some Pilates videos and studios can include New Age components, but this is unusual. After reading this chapter, you should be equipped to recognize those components and find classes that are only fitness related. You might also enjoy stretching classes. If you are looking for online resources, I highly recommend Pietra Fitness,[18] which is a Catholic online workout studio that offers a full video library of workouts aimed at helping you grow stronger in mind, body, and soul as a Catholic. You might also consider an older but similar Christian program called WholyFit.[19]

* * *

Christians throughout history have Christianized, or baptized, certain pagan practices. For example, if you visit a church and see stained-glass windows, you will likely see halos around the heads of Jesus and the saints. The image of the halo was originally used in the Roman Empire to denote divinity.[20] Christians incorporated that imagery into their art. The halo was first added around the head of Jesus Christ to emphasize his divinity and to help lead pagans to the true Lord of heaven and earth. In time, the halo came to indicate simply greatness, or prominence for those who were heroic or deserved to be remembered. Consequently, the Catholic Church extended the use of halos to images of the saints to accentuate their holy, heroic lives.

Some wonder if yoga can be similarly Christianized, but this is not possible. Why? Because yoga is a full system of beliefs and practices that are incompatible with our Christian faith. The main purpose of baptizing a pagan practice is to lead pagans from their limited understanding of God to the fullness of truth, found in Jesus Christ. In other words, evangelization is always the goal. It has never been simply a matter of liking a pagan practice and wishing to partake in it, as is common today.

Moreover, as the Church adopted and Christianized certain pagan practices, the names of those practices were almost always changed so as not to lead people astray. This is why "Christian yoga" is confusing and not actually yoga. In attempts to Christianize practices in our day, teachers who have good intentions often keep the practices virtually the same and even retain the names. Because yoga cannot be Christianized, Christians who claim to practice yoga, even holy yoga, are often heavily influenced by it without knowing it. I encourage you to stay away from anything called "yoga." Enjoy alternative means of exercise, instead, and if you practice the postures and stretches, do not call your exercise "yoga," because it's not. If a practice is called "yoga," it is best to avoid it.

CHAPTER 6
THE TRUTH ABOUT REIKI

Over the last couple of decades, the field of "holistic health" has exploded. Many people actively seek to live healthier lifestyles, focusing on healthy foods, natural remedies, and spiritual practices. Many of these observances pose no problem to our faith. Others do, such as the practice of Reiki and other forms of energy medicine, including Therapeutic Touch, Healing Touch, Hands of Light, and Qigong. Energy medicine has been rapidly gaining acceptance in North America, in hospitals, clinics, and even private practices. Reiki is found even in some Catholic hospitals.

Very simply put, Reiki is purported to be a system of healing based on the belief that everything in the universe is made up of energy. This energy exists all around us.

The system was founded in Japan in 1922 by the Buddhist monk Dr. Mikao Usui.[1] Usui was on a twenty-one-day spiritual retreat, practicing long hours of meditation each day. As the story goes, during one meditation session, the great Reiki Energy of the universe descended into his crown chakra (the energy center in his head) and bestowed upon him the ability to heal people without draining his own life-force energy. A few styles of Reiki existed before Dr. Usui, but they fell into disuse over time. The dominant form of Reiki that people know and use today is Usui

Reiki Ryoho. Dr. Usui himself trained more than 2,000 students and sixteen teachers.[2] Reiki would spread, evolve, and eventually come to the West. It did not become popular in the West until the late twentieth century, however, and along the way it underwent many changes and additions.[3]

The belief surrounding Reiki is summarized by the world-renowned International Center for Reiki Training:

> We are alive because life force is flowing through us. Life force flows within the physical body through pathways called chakras. It also flows around us in a field of energy called the aura. Negative thoughts and feelings attach themselves to the energy field and cause a disruption in the flow of life force. Reiki heals by flowing through the affected parts of the energy field and charging them with positive energy. ... This causes the negative energy to break apart and fall away. In so doing, Reiki clears, straightens and heals the energy pathways, thus allowing the life force to flow in a healthy and natural way.[4]

According to this belief system, sickness, depression, and other conditions can be an indication that negative thoughts and feelings have attached themselves to us and blocked our energy pathways, and this causes disease in the body. Therefore, Reiki masters seek to help clear those blocked pathways by channeling positive energy into a person. Reiki sessions last sixty to ninety minutes, during which a practitioner places his hands on or a few inches from the patient's body. The Reiki master then claims to allow energy to flow through his hands into the patient in order to bring about healing and wholeness.

Reiki Is Not Scientific
The spirituality and belief system of Reiki derives from a Buddhist tradition that contains many beliefs incompatible with

Christianity. We will return to this point later, but let's first address the nature of the energy and other pseudoscientific claims within Reiki. Reiki supporters assert that it is a complementary medicine that works wonders for those who receive it, that it has no negative side effects, and that it is scientifically proven. In reality, the healing effectiveness of Reiki is often highly exaggerated, and the scientific claims remain unproven.

Nobody seems to know the nature of the energy that Reiki practitioners claim to channel to patients. It has been broadly described as a spiritual energy pervading the universe, which we cannot detect or quantify and really know nothing about. It is also said to have a mind of its own. This is in stark contrast to the physical energies that science can detect and measure and work with.

Reiki energy is not accepted by science and is more of a spiritual belief. There is, however, a quantifiable physical energy that is scientific and can be proven. This is called *veritable* energy. Veritable energy is physical energy, and in medicine it uses mechanical vibrations, specific measurable wavelengths, and frequencies to treat patients.[5] Sound and electromagnetic forces (i.e., magnetism, visible light) are two examples of this type of energy.

Conversely, "spiritual" energy, also known as "life-force energy," is said to exist throughout the universe, making up everything. This is referred to as *putative* energy, or an energy that is assumed to exist but cannot be detected and is without verifiable proof. Yet Reiki practitioners allege that this energy exists and forms auras and energy fields and knows how to direct itself to heal people. This practice cannot be authenticated by science because nobody can scientifically prove a spiritual, immeasurable, untestable force.

Most Reiki masters themselves do not understand this energy they purport to use. I interviewed several Reiki masters and other energy healers for this book, and much of the information I received was relative, subjective, and contradictory. There was no standard, and not one answer was the same. In one of the final interviews, a practitioner told me, "If you ask ten different Reiki masters these same questions, you will receive ten different answers. ... It comes down to doing whatever feels right to you."

One of the principal international authorities on Reiki, William Lee Rand,[6] has attempted to prove the scientific nature of Reiki. He mentions all sorts of scientific terms and concepts, but his conclusions are relative and his statements far from conclusive: "The super-consciousness *may* then guide this functioning," "*might* involve special combinations of love," "Scalar waves *may* be responsible for," and so on. In other words, Reiki rests on many theories and conjectures of how these things *might* work or *may* happen, but never anything conclusive.[7]

Science is the empirical study of the natural world, which deals with things that can be observed and tested through hypotheses and repeated experimentation. Therefore, spiritual beliefs and untestable claims remain outside the realm of science. Ironically, even international organizations that actively seek to advance energy medicine and complementary medicine admit that Reiki is *not* scientifically proven and cannot be verified scientifically.

The National Center for Complementary and Alternative Medicine admits that a scientific basis for this spiritual (putative) energy is lacking. Their overview of energy medicine says plainly, "*Putative* energy fields (also called biofields) have defied measurement to date by reproducible methods." It goes on to state that healing methods using putative energy "are among the most controversial of complementary and alternative medicine because neither the external energy fields nor the therapeutic effects have been demonstrated convincingly by any biophysical means."[8]

The Foundation for the Advancement of Energy Medicine similarly states: "Due to the lack of quantifiable evidence of these purported energies, therapies based on putative energy are more controversial. The postulated energies are claimed to be of a more subtle nature and have not been directly measured by reproducible methods."[9]

Likewise, the National Center for Complementary and Integrative Health says, "Several groups of experts have evaluated the evidence on Reiki, and all of them have concluded that it's uncertain whether Reiki is helpful. ... There isn't any scientific evidence that such an energy exists."[10]

Medical News Today admits that "controversy surrounds Reiki, because it is hard to prove its effectiveness through scientific means."[11] Reiki promoters cite different studies to bolster the case for energy medicine, but they leave aside the many scientific, controlled studies that have disproven Reiki and shown it to have little effect. Dr. William J. Jarvis of the National Council Against Health Fraud has stated several times that energy medicine has no basis in science, has yielded few results, and shows nothing more than a placebo effect for patients.[12]

Here is the real test. In 1996, the James Randi Educational Foundation advertised that it would give $742,000 to anyone who could prove the existence of this spiritual energy or exhibit an ability to detect a human energy field under controlled studies. Only one person accepted the test and failed to prove anything. The organization then raised the promised compensation to $1,000,000; it remained unclaimed for years until Randi's retirement.[13]

Even if someone could demonstrate an invisible, conscious energy, scientific evidence would still not justify the use of Reiki for Christians. Of much greater concern, however, are the spiritual beliefs and practices of Reiki, which are incompatible with our faith.

Reiki Is Not Christian

Energy medicine poses serious problems for Christians. Reiki masters make a number of claims that contradict the Bible and basic Christian beliefs. Some of these claims include: God is energy; Reiki energy comes directly from God; God is the universe; Reiki is compatible with every religion; spirits on the other side can help guide the energy; Jesus was a Reiki master.[14] To discern the half-truths and falsities here, we need to unpack the differences between Reiki and Christianity.

First, the God that is posited by Reiki is vastly different from the Christian God. Proponents of Reiki claim that God is energy. They argue that, since energy cannot be created or destroyed,[15] it is eternal. They then conclude that since God is eternal, and energy is eternal, God must be energy. Similarly, since energy pervades the universe, God and the universe must be the same thing. This concept of an unseen, all-pervasive, spiritual energy is a Hindu and Buddhist concept, not a Christian one.

In Hinduism, the god Brahman not only created the universe but *is* the universe. He has infused himself into every last part of creation so that there is no difference between Brahman and his creation.[16] Shakti is the Hindu goddess of energy, and her energy pervades everything.[17] In stark contrast, there is only one God in Christianity. He is not an impersonal energy force, but a Trinity of Persons and a relational Being. God brought the universe into existence out of nothing (see Gn 1:1; Col 1:16; Jn 1:1–3), and he transcends his creation. This means that while God is present among us, he is not part of the universe in any way, and the universe is not a part of him. So, Christian Reiki practitioners who postulate that God is energy or part of the universe are taking from Hinduism and have a flawed understanding of their Creator.

Another point of departure between Christianity and Reiki is their beliefs about what gives human beings life. Like many Eastern religions, Reiki posits the existence of a life-force energy (also known as *chi*, *ki*, or *qui*) that fills the universe and surrounds us at all times. This life-force energy is said to give us life and is considered to be the life-giving agent. Conversely, Christians teach that God is the Creator of all life and has made us a composite of body and soul. Consequently, it is the *soul* that is our spiritual life-giving principle, not life-force energy. The

Catholic Church teaches infallibly that God has personally given each and every person a soul. Throughout Scripture, the soul is mentioned numerous times, but the teaching on energy cannot be found anywhere. This can also be said of chakras, auras, biofields, energy fields, and many other analogous beliefs.[18]

Another major difference between Christianity and Reiki is in regard to our Lord. Claims that Jesus was a Reiki master are erroneous, as they make him just another enlightened guru and not the Lord of all. Yet some Christians accept and teach this falsity. In reality, Jesus is the only eternal and unbegotten Son of God. He shares the same divine nature as God the Father and thus possesses the same infinite power as his Father. This means that during his life on earth, Jesus, because he was God, could heal anybody at any time from any illness or disease. Jesus was not a Reiki master and did not channel unseen energy into sick people in order to heal them. Rather, he healed them by his own power as God. No Reiki master in history could heal as Jesus healed, because no Reiki master is God almighty. The claim that Jesus had anything to do with Reiki is preposterous — especially since Reiki did not exist until many centuries after Christ.

Jesus' apostles were not Reiki masters either. They laid hands on people and healed them instantly by the power of God. They never stood over sick people to channel unseen energy into their bodies but healed them instantly by the power of Jesus. Pore over the pages of the Bible and research the more than 2,000 years of Catholic teaching, and you will find no Reiki teachings there. Quite simply, Reiki is not a Christian belief or practice, and the two are incompatible with each other.

As mentioned earlier, studies, trials, and experiments regarding Reiki, Therapeutic Touch, and other energy-medicine techniques reveal that the practices have little or no effect on patients, other than subjectively or emotionally.[19] In my interviews with energy healers, I inquired about the effects of Reiki on their patients. Were their clients healed? Many of the answers I received were the same: Patients were not healed, but Reiki

gave them a better outlook on life or a greater feeling of acceptance. (This is in contrast to many more scientific studies that
have been performed showing little or no difference.)[20] So, while
Reiki may provide some short-term, subjective relief to patients,
in general it has not been proven to provide lasting healing.

Psychologically, for a person to have somebody there to love
him and pay attention to him is healing and creates positive results in his mind and his emotions.[21] And these results can be
achieved in other ways that are consistent with Christian faith.
Some alternatives may include counseling, massage, or just having someone spend time with a patient and offer a friendly ear.
People need to be loved. Many times, just being touched or paid
attention to can have a therapeutic effect. This has nothing to
with a supposed life-force energy, chakras, or anything like that.
It's simply rooted in our human nature and our need for connection with others.

True Christian healing has nothing to do with energy. Just
consider the miracles of the saints or genuine Christian healers today. In Jesus' name, they heal people, help people, and
sometimes even perform astounding miracles. Not all of these
healings are immediate, but the fruit is undeniable, and the approach is in line with God and his teachings. Christians with the
gift of healing do not just relieve stress or help people to become
more calm or accept their circumstances. They offer real healing
through Jesus Christ.

One notable example is Sister Briege McKenna, from Ire-
land, who is an internationally renowned healer. Sister McKenna
recounts in her book *Miracles Do Happen*: "I went to a hospital
and prayed for a woman who was dying of cancer. The doctors
had said there was no hope. On my way out, I noticed this poor
man suffering with shingles, and I prayed with him. The woman,
a few days later, went home from the hospital in perfect health.
And the man with shingles was healed too."[22]

Worldwide healer Father Fernando Suarez, and others like
him, also heal people from many ailments, as Jesus did and in a

manner consistent with Christianity. Many saints had this gift. One of my favorites is Saint André Bessette, from Montreal, Canada, who had miraculous powers through faith in Jesus. He is famous for healing people from all kinds of diseases. After he died, even people who touched his coffin were completely healed from incurable ailments.

So, what is the difference between Christian healing and Reiki? Jesuit scholar Father Mitch Pacwa states, "Praying for the sick has to be understood as an aspect of God's grace operating in our lives. It's not a 'technique.' That's where it becomes 'magical,' and Christianity is not about using magic." Kathleen McCarthy, who was involved in a charismatic healing ministry for thirty-three years, explains the differences between the charismatic gift of healing and Reiki:

> In the charismatic gift of healing and the laying on of hands, the hands are just a symbol of service. We are not acting as a channel. We are not a conduit for any energy. We are instruments of God's healing. ... Our hands are just an outward sign showing this person that we are joining with them in prayer. ... Thinking that we can participate in these [other] practices simply by believing that the energy comes from God is a dangerous delusion, particularly in the case of techniques such as Reiki, which employs "attunement" rituals involving secret symbols and the use of spirit guides.[23]

In his book *An Exorcist Tells His Story*, Father Amorth writes, "If healing occurs through energy that the healer transfers to the sick person, either through psychic charge or through a different store of energy, it has nothing to do with charismatic healing. Additionally, there may be a danger of evil infiltration. That is why we need extreme prudence."[24] So, Reiki and healing with energy are not from God and can even be from a demonic source. In addition, Reiki has the possibility of opening one up to a demonic influence, a point we will return to.

Often Christians who are duped by Reiki or Healing Touch are pulled in by ignorance, lack of catechesis, or a sincere desire to heal people but in the wrong manner. This includes the many Catholic sisters and religious who practice Reiki and believe that God is working through them. While their intentions may be noble, they are deceived.

Reiki and the Occult

In addition to the problematic elements already mentioned, there are many additional occult and New Age influences that are often part of Reiki practices. These include spirit guides, talking to beings on "the other side," the "higher Self," past-life regression, psychic experiences, crystals, secret knowledge, and healing symbols.

The process of becoming a Reiki master involves training, usually in various levels of Reiki school. Then, before becoming a master, one must receive an *attunement*, which is said to be like turning the dial of a radio from static to a station that comes in clearly. It is believed that this process opens up the Reiki practitioner to higher frequencies of life-force energy, which is transmitted from the master to the student.

Regarding attunements, the International Center for Reiki Training states:

> Reiki is a special kind of life force that can only be channeled by someone that has been attuned to it. ... It is transferred to the student by the Reiki master during an attunement process. This process opens the crown, heart, and palm chakras and creates a special link between the student and the Reiki source. ... This process is guided by the Reiki or God consciousness and makes adjustments in the process depending on the needs of each student. The attunement is also attended by Reiki guides and other spiritual beings who help implement

the process. Many report having mystical experiences involving personal messages, healings, visions, and past life experiences. The attunement can also increase your psychic sensitivity.[25]

To any faithful Christian, this should raise a number of warning signals. You may have noticed the mention of chakras, past-life experiences, spirit guides, psychic sensitivities, and other beings who attend the ceremony. Reiki proponents assert that there are no negative effects with the use of energy medicine. Exorcists and others disagree. Clearly, this practice opens the way for a number of dangerous spiritual influences, including demonic activity.

Many people who undergo Reiki complain of ill effects that range from feeling sick to demonic activity.[26] I once received a phone call from a middle-aged woman across the country. She began going to Reiki sessions to receive healing. The opposite happened. She revealed the demonic attacks that were occurring and the harassment she felt constantly. I recommended her to an exorcist along with some deliverance prayers. This poor woman is not alone in her experience of Reiki. I have heard from numerous people who recount demonic activity, attacks, and other ill effects after they began Reiki.

Some practitioners who leave the practice of energy medicine also report needing demonic deliverance. Some years back, a priest told me that he was called in to exorcise an entire convent of religious sisters who had practiced Reiki and were suffering from demonic activity. Moira Noonan, a former Reiki master, needed several hours of demonic deliverance after she left the practice. As she recounts in her book *Ransomed from Darkness*:

> Another psychic healing system I was involved with was Reiki. Reiki is a method of healing through the transmission and activation of a person's energy. This therapy looks somewhat like the Christian laying on of

hands, but this is deceptive. ... When I mentioned Reiki, Father Philip Pavich knew the forces I was talking about. He actually knew the names of [the demon] and other spirits that were attached to Reiki. He knew [the demon] and his crew were adversaries of the Holy Spirit, and he was able to deliver me from them. ... I saw more clearly than ever how every occult practice has a demon attached to it.[27]

These are only some of the reasons why Catholic bishops have outright condemned Reiki and do not allow Catholics to participate in it. In the document "Guidelines for Evaluating Reiki as an Alternative Therapy," the bishops state, "It is inappropriate for Catholic institutions, such as Catholic health care facilities and retreat centers, or persons representing the church, such as chaplains, to promote or provide support for Reiki Therapy."[28] I encourage you to read the whole document, available at USCCB. org, for more information. One cannot be a "good Catholic" and practice Reiki. Some Catholics have tried, but an overview of their writings reveals that they have fallen prey to counterfeit spiritual beliefs and ideologies.

In light of the bishops' statement, some Catholics who practice Reiki have attempted to disguise the practice by changing the name to "relaxation massage," "massage healing," or some similarly ambiguous term. Others claim that the bishops' statement is lacking. It is important to arm yourself with information about this practice, so you know how to avoid it. Know also that, if you have the desire to help people find healing, this is a good thing. Trust that God can work numerous blessings in and through you. Do not stop desiring to help people! Ask God to show you ways of accomplishing this goal that are compatible with our faith and in line with what the Church teaches.

CHAPTER 7
CENTERING PRAYER

Many people mistake fake "designer" purses, clothing, or antiques for the real thing. Although they look similar, they are cheap knockoffs, worth only a fraction of the price of actual designer goods. In the realm of spirituality, the same thing can happen. Counterfeit spiritual practices may mimic authentic ones, looking and seeming the same, but they are not the real thing and will not bring us closer to God. This is the case with modern-day centering prayer, which looks like Christian prayer but is not.

What is Christian prayer? Our Catholic Faith teaches that prayer is lifting our minds and hearts to God in love. It is our way to foster and cultivate a relationship with our Lord and Savior Jesus Christ. Prayer consists of talking to God and listening to him, meditating on him and reflecting on his Word, and, through this, coming to know him on a deeper level. What is the goal of prayer? Love! Prayer consists of nothing less than a deep, intimate, personal, loving relationship with Almighty God, who is very much in love with each one of us. Keep this in mind as we proceed.

Centering prayer is becoming a popular practice in the Western world, and it can be difficult to tell when such prayer is authentically Christian and when it is not. Sadly, most of the centering-prayer movements found in Catholic retreat centers and parishes today in the United States are the counterfeit version. Consequently, those who fall into these practices in their sincere desire to grow closer to God are being led astray. How can we tell the difference and avoid the counterfeit version of prayer?

We must begin by examining the acceptable and more ancient form of "centering" prayer practiced by many Eastern Catholics. In this practice, a person repeats a one-line prayer, called the Jesus Prayer, which says: "Jesus, Son of the living God, have mercy on me, a sinner." The person repeats this prayer many times throughout the day, while busy, at work, or at rest. It is common to recite the first half of the prayer while breathing in slowly and the second half while gently exhaling. Saying this prayer throughout the day allows a person to keep Jesus constantly present in his mind and on his heart. Ideally, one meditates and reflects on these words, contemplating God's love and mercy. Anytime those who embrace this practice become overly distracted in life or in prayer, they can return to the Jesus Prayer to center themselves again on what is most important in their lives: Jesus Christ. It keeps them in the presence of God; their whole goal is to keep their minds and hearts filled with love for the Lord. In other words, they stay centered on him.

This is not dissimilar to the practice of choosing a daily Bible verse to repeat throughout the day. Alternately, some choose a prayer of praise or thanksgiving, such as, "I love you, Jesus. Thank you for your immense love." They repeat this prayer throughout the day in order to keep their minds and hearts focused on God and his presence. The saints practiced the presence of God as well. Whether they were at work or at prayer, they focused on God's presence in and around them. After all, that is what lovers do: They think of each other often and find joy in it.

The modern-day centering-prayer movement has a very different goal. Its aim is not to fill the mind with God, but to empty the mind completely. The practice, as it is used among Catholics today, was founded by Father Thomas Keating,[1] with the help of Father Basil Pennington and Father William Meninger.

It reflects a Hindu and Buddhist spirituality, attempting to fuse these religions with Christianity. In this practice, a person empties his or her mind of all thoughts. The focus is on emptying and more emptying, which is the opposite of the authentically Christian form of centering prayer. The Vatican document "On Some Aspects of Christian Meditation" speaks to this: "Naturally we want to forget the world to concentrate solely on God, but the various emptying techniques don't go this far. They stop at the emptying and the emptying becomes the goal."[2]

In his book *Open Mind, Open Heart*, Keating teaches a theology very similar to the Hindu concept that man and God are the same. He writes, "God and our true Self are not separate. Though we are not God, God and our true Self are the same thing."[3] He states in another place, "The first part of the Christian journey is to realize that there is an Other. The second part is to become the Other. The third and greatest part is to realize that *there is no Other*."[4] Keating capitalizes the word "Self," hinting that our true self is a divine Self.[5] This is deeply problematic, harkening to a famous saying in Hinduism: "Atman is Brahman, and Brahman is Atman" or "God is my soul, and my soul is God." This is not Christianity but pantheism.[6]

The Vatican released a document on the New Age movement and false spiritual beliefs, titled *Jesus Christ, the Bearer of the Water of Life*. This document specifically states that God is always other: "New Age mysticism is turning inwards on oneself rather than communion with God who is 'totally other.' It is fusion with the universe, an ultimate annihilation of the individual in the unity of the whole."[7] Moreover, "it is necessary in the first place to bear in mind that man is essentially a creature, and remains such for eternity, so that an absorbing of the human self into the divine self is never possible, not even in the highest states of grace."[8]

Authentic prayer involves praying to God, listening to him, and reflecting and meditating on him. Ultimately, prayer is having a relationship with God, which means filling ourselves with him. Centering prayer, as it is practiced in today, leads away from this goal. In fact, the goal of this form of prayer is to reach a mental void, a state of zero or complete nothingness, where one "consents to God."[9]

If our goal in prayer is to sit quietly with all of our attention and focus on the presence of God in or around us, that is good. But if the goal is to sit with a completely empty mind, a void, then we should reject this kind of prayer. Clearing your mind can be utilized as a preparation for prayer and meditation, but it should never be a substitution for prayer. Quieting our thoughts for prayer and trying to silence our wandering minds is a good thing. To rid our minds entirely of all words and thoughts, however, even ones that God offers, is a flawed method of prayer. Remember, the goal of prayer is relationship. And although Father Keating is seeking this through centering prayer, his method has many flaws, as we will see.

Compare the modern method of centering prayer with a husband who desires to cultivate a deeper relationship with his wife. To attain this, he ventures into a quiet corner of his house to spend the next twenty minutes repeating a word to diminish all distraction. This includes all thoughts of his wife, his own actions, their relationship, any loving words she may have said, everything. If something beautiful, edifying, or helpful for the relationship enters his mind, he will immediately remove it and return to the word. In attempting to love his wife more, he intentionally does not speak to her, contemplate her, or entertain a single thought about her in order to improve their relationship. He merely sits in silence, consenting.

Would it not be better quietly to remove all thoughts *except* those of his wife and his marriage? From there, he could reflect on what is good, what is bad, what he needs to work on, the ways he can love his wife more, and so on. In this way, his contemplation would naturally lead him closer to his wife during and after the meditation time, and even lead him to a silent time in which he can simply reflect deeply.

Let us imagine a healthier scenario. Imagine these same lovers facing each other and holding hands, staring deeply and lovingly into each other's eyes. They continue to stare quietly with a profound focus, and not a single word is said. They remain enchanted and captivated by each other. Their minds are totally quiet and at peace, just taking in the wonder of the other. They are not thinking about the laundry, the kids, or the long to-do list. Rather, their minds are completely focused and totally centered on each other in the moment. Love is flowing in and out of their hearts and is being shared between them. That is what contemplative prayer with God looks like. It does not resemble Centering Prayer, which would be more like the same couple closing their eyes and trying to remove the other person from their thoughts, trying to focus on each other by focusing on nothing.

Again, learning to quiet our wandering minds and eliminate distractions is a good and necessary thing, for mental focus can only make us better lovers. But to rid ourselves entirely of all thoughts and then call this emptiness "prayer" is very different. There is nothing wrong with taking time before prayer to quiet our thoughts in order to focus our attention on God and his presence. Using a repeated word or phrase for a short time to help us calm our minds is acceptable too, as long as it is a prayerful word or phrase that can help lead us into prayer with God.

Centering Prayer Is Not Contemplation

Contemplative prayer (or infused prayer, or prayer of the heart) is the deepest form of prayer, which leads to union with God. It is something given to us by God; we cannot achieve it on our own, particularly not through practical techniques.

In fact, we cannot "practice contemplation" at will by merely using a technique.[10] The journey to contemplative prayer is a long one, involving time, sacrifice, meditation, purification from sin, and growth in holiness. There are no shortcuts. Father Thomas Dubay, an expert on prayer, warns: "One should beware of techniques for emptying the mind to prepare it for contemplation. This is unnatural. Our minds are meant to be filled, not emptied. Nowhere does Scripture advise this. Rather, the beginner is told to fill his mind by pondering the word of God day and night (Ps 1:1–2)."[11]

The great saints and mystics teach us that deep prayer comes only through holiness of life and a deepening of our relationship with God. The journey to contemplative prayer begins with vocal prayer and moves to meditative prayer, which involves reading, thinking, imagining, reflecting, and conversing inwardly with God. After great faithfulness to this form of prayer, God himself — in his own time and his own way — begins to infuse his very life and love, his presence, into the soul. In other words, God begins to give prayer to us on a much deeper level. Simultaneously, our minds become much less active and far quieter and more passive. Yet the meditations are deeper and more invisible and intense. We eventually become quiet interiorly. We may have short or long periods of this "prayer of quiet," in which we are solely focused on the presence of God in or around us.

This is when we will experience contemplative prayer if we are faithful. "Infused contemplation is a divinely given, general, non-conceptual, loving awareness of God. There are no images, no concepts, no ideas, no visions. Sometimes this awareness of God takes the form of a loving attention, sometimes of a dry desire, sometimes of a strong thirsting. None of these experiences is the result of reading or reasoning — they are given, received. The infusion is serene, purifying. It can be delicate or brief, or in advanced stages, burning, powerful, absorbing, prolonged."[12]

In this very advanced stage of prayer, a person does not think, reflect, or ponder in any way. His mind is very still, quiet, attentive, and entirely enraptured in God or in an awareness of his presence. It may take different forms. Sometimes the awareness of God's presence is so real, a person can feel it. One may experience the love of God in an overflowing, tangible way. His love is close, strong, intimate, filling every fiber of one's being. A person does not *do* anything; he just *is* — perfectly focused on God while God is entirely focused on him. This is a love relationship at the deepest level.

Other times, contemplation can be a profound supernatural infusion of peace or joy. This could last a minute, an hour, or, in some cases, days. It can be brief and light or intense, prolonged, and powerful. During this time, the mind is far from empty. Even when this type of prayer takes the form of a "dry desire,"[13] and the person feels estranged from God, he desires closeness to God with his whole heart, mind, and soul, though it is painful and trying. The person thirsts more than anything to be close to God, even though he does not feel it. In true contemplative prayer, one's attention is always on the Lord, and it never leaves him even for the slightest moment until the infusion is finished.

Some people worry that sitting in silence before God without saying or doing anything cannot really be prayer. This is untrue. In fact, just being with God, focused on his presence in and around you, without saying anything, leads to the deepest, most intimate prayer communion with God. Without interior silence, we remain stunted in our spiritual lives. Centering Prayer does well in seeking interior silence in its practice, but the silence it seeks is more of an empty void akin to Buddhism, not a mental silence filled with the presence of God.

Centering Prayer and other such practices are "ultimately an appeal to one's own ability to reach the divine." True prayer, on the other hand, is ultimately meant to be "a meeting with God."[14] This is backed up by the great saints and mystics of the Church, who came face-to-face with God through prayer. Saints such as Teresa of Ávila and John of the Cross, for example, teach us that we must sit before God for *his* sake, expecting nothing and demanding nothing. We must just sit lovingly and attentively in his divine presence with our whole focus upon him. This is very different from the goal of Centering Prayer, which is to achieve emptiness. God is found in silence, but not in emptiness of mind.

Prayer is not about feelings or what we get out of it. It is about having a relationship with God. This relationship with God is like a marital covenant, in which, as lovers, we choose to love each other and be there for each other even when it is a sacrifice or when we do not feel like it. Over time, sitting before the Lord in silence transforms us. Just having the opportunity and the privilege to be there in his presence out of love is enough. We look at him. He looks at us.

CHAPTER 8

A MAZE OF CONFUSION: THE ENNEAGRAM AND LABYRINTHS

Two practices that have been popular in Catholic circles are the Enneagram and labyrinths. The Enneagram was extremely popular in the late 1900s and still is today in some circles, though less so. Labyrinths continue to grow in popularity, and more people are discovering them. Each of these practices has some truth attached to it, but each also reflects many problematic aspects that Christians should be aware of. In this chapter, we will learn to discern between what is good and what is not.

The Enneagram
Since the 1970s, proponents of the Enneagram have claimed that this practice helps people to grow and become the best people they can be, by providing a wealth of insight into their personalities. Though less common today than in its heyday, the Enneagram is still very popular in some Catholic circles. It is likely to be encountered at many Catholic retreat centers, in parishes, and online, as well as in other contexts.

The Enneagram is a system based on different religious traditions, pseudo-psychology, and the occult. It is "a geometric figure that maps out the nine fundamental personality types of human nature and their complex relationships."[1] The word "enneagram" means "nine," and the whole system is allegedly based on nine deadly sins that human beings struggle with (even though Christianity lists only seven deadly sins). Correspondingly, the Enneagram posits that there are nine personality types, which are alleged to be the nine "faces of God" in creation.[2]

How does it work? Each person has a dominant personality type (symbolized by a number, as shown in the diagram below). Each type has strengths and weaknesses. For example, according to Enneagram teaching, number-8-type people want to be in control of their lives but are also aggressive and controlling of others. So, the goal is to follow the numbers in the right order to corresponding personality types to balance yourself out and find wholeness. This will enable you to become one with yourself and others and will help you to uncover your true divine nature.

There are a number of problems with the Enneagram for Catholics, and what follows is only a brief treatment. See the resources section at the end of this book for further materials on this practice and how Catholics should approach and view it.

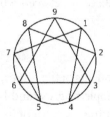

To begin, there is a difference between the symbol itself and the personality types associated with it, but both are steeped in the occult. It is said that the Enneagram (depicted above) was brought into the modern world by a man named George Ivanovich Gurdjieff in the 1900s. From a very young age, Gurdjieff was fascinated by "esoteric knowledge," and he spent much of his life traveling the world to study different cultures and "wisdom traditions."[3] At some point, he claimed to have come across the Enneagram symbol and eventually developed a system to teach on it. He pulled from various religious traditions, including Christianity, Cabbala,* and the occult. Gurdjieff boldly taught that no one could understand anything completely, including one's place in this world, except in terms of the Enneagram.[4] This symbol, however, had nothing to do with personality types when Gurdjieff used it. That would originate in the mind of a man named Oscar Ichazo.

Like Gurdjieff, Ichazo was interested in esoteric knowledge and traveled the world to discover it. He also pulled from many religions, cultures, and philosophies, including the occult, which helped lay the foundation for his teachings on the Enneagram. The ideas of the nine personality types are said to have originated in ancient Greece, and they can allegedly be traced down through the centuries. Ichazo systematized them for the first time in the mid-1950s, when he included them in his teaching on the Enneagram.

In his book *Catholics and the New Age*, Father Mitch Pacwa confirms that Ichazo lived a life of pagan spiritualism: astrology, Zen, Cabbala, Shamanism, psychedelic drugs, Native American spirituality, and hypnotism were all part of his life. Ichazo also frequently practiced divination, contacting spirits and receiving instruction through higher spirits.[5] For this reason, Father Pacwa states that "Christians need to be aware of the enneagram's occult origins so they can prevent occult traces from infecting their faith in Jesus Christ."[6]

The other person responsible for establishing the Enneagram as we know it today was a psychiatrist named Claudio Naranjo. In the early 1970s, Naranjo traveled to Chile to study with Ichazo. He brought his teachings back to the United States

---

* A New Age form of Jewish mysticism.

and expanded the practice based on some of his studies of psychology. He trained and instructed many students, who went on to teach others. From there, the Enneagram began to grow in popularity, spreading even into Christian churches.

Some claim that the Enneagram we know today is hundreds of years old, but this is not true. Father Pacwa states that there is no evidence to support this, and the nine personality types outlined in the practice do not go "back any farther than Ichazo in the 1960s. Neither Gurdjieff nor his disciples write about it."[7]

Many sincere Christians attempt to utilize the Enneagram as a purely psychological tool, but the Enneagram's psychological aspects cannot be divorced from its occultic origins.

There are other issues with the Enneagram as well. As mentioned earlier, it teaches that there are nine deadly sins, while our faith teaches that there are only seven. According to Enneagram teaching and philosophy, the Devil is not real, hell is a myth, and sin does not exist. These teachings, of course, are contrary to the Catholic Faith. When the Enneagram is used in Catholic circles, practitioners teach that the Devil is not Satan, but a person's ego, while hell means "living in the ego." The goal of the Enneagram, even in Catholic settings, is to move out of the deadly sins and into one's "true identity."

The Enneagram may use Christian terminology, but it is not a Christian practice. In a sense, the Enneagram is also seen as a means of salvation and personal freedom that we do all the work to achieve. The problem is that this removes the truth about where our salvation and freedom come from: Jesus Christ. By his death and resurrection, he saves us from sin, frees us, and gives us meaning, fulfillment, and eternal life. He alone is the way to heaven; we cannot achieve heaven on our own or through any man-made system, such as the Enneagram.

There is even an Enneagram "prayer" that encapsulates many of the problematic spiritual elements that contradict our faith. This prayer, like many beliefs that surround the Enneagram, replaces the eternal, all-powerful God with his creation.

In other words, it is the universe that provides for us, that gives us what we need, and that gives "eternal life." The prayer also equates our nature with the "Universal Source" and claims that we are perfect.[8]

The Enneagram attempts to meld various types of spirituality with psychology. Leaving aside the troubling aspects of the spiritual beliefs associated with it, the Enneagram does not deal with hard psychological science. Rather, its focus has been on occult spirituality and on the cosmos. Although the Enneagram may include some helpful information regarding personality traits, it is not a helpful psychological tool. If it were, why would there not be numerous scientific studies demonstrating its effectiveness? The Christian Research Institute has raised these questions:

> What *psychological* proof do they have that only nine basic types exist? And what is the evidence that these are in fact the correct nine? This has not been researched. … What is the evidence that a resentful perfectionist (one) should seek the virtue of the happy-go-lucky planner (seven)? Why should the vengeful, power-hungry person (eight) become a helper (two) rather than seek other virtues? Besides faith in the antiquity of the system, which it does not possess, how can anyone know the best virtues to pursue for any individual type? No research has been done in this regard, yet enneagram experts suggest specific spiritual goals based on this system to their students in parishes and retreat houses. The lack of scientific study should set off alarms for anyone interested in this approach to spiritual growth.[9]

For these and many other reasons, the Catholic Church does not endorse the Enneagram. In fact, the Church's document on New Age spirituality specifically warns that the Enneagram is a false form of Christian spirituality and a type of Gnosticism that has its roots in divination.[10] Christians should stay away from this practice and stick with Myers-Briggs or other personality tests that are rooted in sound psychology and do not contain problematic spiritual elements.

The Labyrinth

Labyrinths are similar to mazes. In mazes, one often gets lost before finding his way out. Labyrinths similarly have a beginning point, from which one must find the end by following a path. Labyrinths date back thousands of years and have multiple meanings and purposes, depending on the country and the culture in which they are used, ranging from stories of Greek mythology to structures built as parts of tombs for kings.[11]

Christian labyrinths emerged in the thirteenth century, allowing people to make spiritual pilgrimages when unable to embark on physical journeys to the Holy Land. The modern Christian use of the labyrinth, however, includes many troubling ties to New Age spirituality. This brief overview is designed to help you to discern the difference between Christian labyrinths and those that involve elements incompatible with Christian belief.

Throughout the history of the Church, Christians have been encouraged to make pilgrimages to the Holy Land. During the Middle Ages, however, this was a very long, arduous journey for Christians in Europe. In addition, there were fears of Muslim attacks, and the trip was very expensive. So, whether due to safety concerns, poor health, financial issues, or other obstacles, many Christians could not make a pilgrimage to Jerusalem, as they desired. Thus, Christian labyrinths were created. Pilgrims would walk through a maze with the same purpose and intention that a pilgrimage to the Holy Land would entail: praying, doing penance, and seeking to draw closer to God. The most famous of these mazes is at Chartres Cathedral in France.

In contrast, the modern New Age version of the labyrinth is focused on the self. This labyrinth was developed in 1991 by Lauren Artress, an Episcopalian priest at Grace Cathedral

Church in San Francisco. She devoted more than twenty years to popularizing and promoting the labyrinth to people around the world.[12] Her books and teachings led to what is known as the "the Labyrinth Movement,"[13] which has become quite popular in Christian and some Catholic circles.

Although Artress based her labyrinth on the popular Catholic version at Chartres, her labyrinth is not a Christian one but a New Age counterfeit, void of authentic Christian spirituality. Artress's beliefs that underlie her labyrinth were influenced by the occult, goddess spirituality, and the Human Potential Movement.[14] This will be seen in more detail below.

Today, most Christian retreat centers across the country have labyrinths based on Artress's New Age version, not the Christian tradition. Like Grace Cathedral, much of the literature and online explanations use Christian language but do not have Christian meaning. Instead, they are rooted in New Age understandings and practices, which can be confusing for unsuspecting participants. How can you tell the difference? By carefully reading descriptions of the labyrinths and their purposes.

In Catholic labyrinths, a person prays specifically to Jesus while meditating on his life. As one walks the path, one meditates on the Passion of Jesus, recites the Stations of the Cross, or reflects on one's own sinfulness. Simultaneously, the person ponders ways to counteract sin, to grow in virtue, and to become holier. On the other hand, with New Age labyrinths, the focus is not on Christ but on self. In her book *Learn to Discern: Is It Christian or New Age?*, former New Age practitioner Susan Brinkmann comments on the differences:

> There are supposedly three stages to walking a labyrinth, all of them bearing names that are associated with Christian mystical tradition, although the meanings are radically different.
>
> For example, the "purgation" stage of the labyrinth walk is described as a *"releasing, a letting go of the details*

of your life" as opposed to the Christian idea of purgation which involves a turning away from sin and em-
bracing the Gospel.

The "illumination" stage of the labyrinth walk is
when one reaches the center of the labyrinth where they
are advised to *"Receive what is there for you to receive."*
In the Christian concept, illumination occurs when one
achieves a new closeness to God after a deeper embrace
of Gospel living.

The unitive stage in labyrinth language is when
one *"is joining God, your Higher Power, or the healing
forces at work in the world."* In the Christian tradition,
this is the stage where the soul has been so purified as
to achieve transforming union with God, the closest a
creature can come to God during their earthly life.[15]

The labyrinth itself is not evil, and when used rightly in accord
with true Christian spirituality, it can be very beneficial. The
best way to discern which kind of labyrinth you're dealing with
is to investigate the spiritual beliefs and practices behind it, as
these dictate whether it is genuine or heterodox. Before you use
a labyrinth, look at the organization's website or read the accom-
panying literature. If a labyrinth is focused on Jesus and conversion, great! If it has vague explanation of nice thoughts that all
revolve around you, it's New Age. The website for Grace Cathedral, discussed above, is an example of a problematic labyrinth.[16]
The website outlines three stages of the labyrinth:

1. Releasing, or leaving behind the trivial things of
   your life and quieting the mind (associated with the
   traditional stage of purgation)
2. Receiving whatever is there for you to receive (associated with illumination)
3. Returning (associated with union)

The site encourages the user, "Each time you walk the labyrinth you become more empowered to find and do the work for which you feel your soul is reaching."[17]

The cathedral's description of its labyrinth contains no mention of Jesus or of sin. The user is encouraged to empty himself of thoughts and distractions, not of sin. There is no mention of purification, repentance, or conversion, which are the goals of a Catholic labyrinth or pilgrimage. Moreover, it does not encourage prayer to Jesus Christ but focuses on the self: emptying oneself, filling oneself, and bringing healing forces into the world. The description contains only a vague notion of God.

* * *

Both the Enneagram and New Age labyrinths have their origins in non-Christian beliefs and the occult. They veer far from authentic Christian spirituality, yet sadly, many sincere Christians who do not know better are duped by them. This is why it is essential that we have a clear understanding of the principles that underly these and other practices, so we can avoid counterfeit spiritualities in our search for authentic practices. In particular, notice where the practice leads: Does it genuinely lead us to God, or does it draw us deeper into ourselves? Or does it merely lead to a higher power? Does it acknowledge the reality of sin, or does it deny or attempt to soften the truth about what sin is? These principles also underlie our discernment of many other Eastern practices, which we will visit in our next chapter as we journey to the East.

CHAPTER 9
EASTERN BELIEFS AND PRACTICES

Zen Buddhism

Many Westerners live life in the fast lane, bogged down by frantic chaos and never-ending busyness. They do not feel fulfilled or at peace. Naturally, then, for those who never stop to smell the roses, the peaceful life can be a draw. And it should be. God intended for us to be at peace, to find fulfillment, and to be in quiet union with him. The practice of Zen Buddhism thus has a lot of appeal for Christians, as on the surface it seems to lead to the same goals.

We cannot deny that Zen Buddhism shares certain truths with Christianity and is able to provide some benefits for living. For example, this spirituality teaches the need for mental discipline, the importance of virtue, and the necessity of living in the present moment. These principles are similar to Christian principles, and we respect them. Zen, however, is not Christianity. In fact, there are drastic differences, and we need to be aware of them so we do not allow ourselves to be taken in by this practice.

In practice, Zen is a form of meditation within Buddhism used to achieve enlightenment. Centering Prayer (discussed in chapter 7) derives a good deal of its method from this practice. Zen consists of long periods of meditation each day, in which a person quiets his mind to achieve a state of complete nothingness.

Father Robert E. Kennedy, a Catholic priest who claims to be a Zen master, confirms this goal of Zen. In his book *Zen Spirit, Christian Spirit*, he states, "The daily twelve hours of *zazen* [the meditation practices in Zen Buddhism] ... helps the retreatant to empty her mind of all thoughts, images, feelings, anxieties, and desires, even of the desire for enlightenment itself. In Zen, the conscious mind must be brought to a standstill and remain in total darkness."[1] (Father Kennedy also acknowledges, "Not all Christians will be interested in practicing Zen because of its disagreement with Christianity on theological and philosophical issues."[2])

The goal of this emptying of the mind is Nirvana, or the ultimate freedom of Self-realization. Zen practitioners believe that this is a realization of the interconnectedness with all of creation, with all that is. Ruben Habito, another Zen master and former Jesuit priest, writes, "The spiritual core is the deepest center of the person. It is here that the person is open to the transcendent dimension. It is here that a person experiences ultimate reality. ... The fourth maxim tells us that what we see is our own true nature. And, seeing this, we become an Awakened One (a Buddha)."[3]

Again, this is not a Christian practice. How can we recognize the disconnect with Christianity? First, most Buddhism does not posit belief in God, much less a personal God. For Buddhists, seeking peace in emptiness poses no problem. For Christians, who believe in a personal and all-powerful Creator who wishes to commune with us, however, seeking to empty the mind is deeply problematic, because it takes us away from union with God, rather than leading us to it.

Second, practitioners of Zen Buddhism strive to reach deeper spiritual levels through their own efforts. In contrast, Christians believe that salvation can be attained only through Jesus Christ, who died to take away our sins. Also, we cannot approach God or grow closer to his divine majesty without the help of his grace and power working in our lives. Even in deeper

Christian meditation and contemplation, God does most of the work as he draws us to himself. Salvation is certainly nothing we can achieve on our own. In contrast, Zen is all about the human experience and everything the human person can do to obtain enlightenment.

Third, Zen Buddhism teaches that people cannot know anything at all through knowledge or reason but only through experience, which is why one must work so hard to empty his mind of all thoughts. According to this practice, truth can never be known, only experienced. As a result, the temptation for Christians who practice Zen is to value personal feelings over commandments and doctrines. For Christians, this is quite dangerous. Seeking to strip all knowledge away for personal, subjective "experiences" (that contradict one another, depending on whom you ask) is not a Christian practice. In fact, it negates the fact that Jesus came to teach us about God and who he is.

Among others, the following principles in Zen Buddhism are irreconcilable for Christians:

- being one with the universe
- equating God with complete nothingness or "emptiness of being"
- mind-emptying and concentration techniques
- void meditative states

Emptying ourselves of everything, including all thoughts, will never help us approach God or cultivate a loving relationship with him. Although the discipline that Zen provides and the virtues that it seeks to cultivate may be admirable, Zen is incompatible with Christian faith.

Transcendental Meditation
Transcendental Meditation (TM) is another form of Eastern meditation. TM was brought to the United States in the 1960s by its founder, Maharishi Mahesh Yogi. Yogi developed his

practice in India, based on ancient Hindu spirituality and scriptures, specifically the *Bhagavad Gita*.[4] TM includes two twenty-
minute periods of meditation per day. This is accomplished
through the use of a mantra in order to quiet the mind. The goal
of this practice is to liberate oneself from pain and suffering, to
achieve enlightenment,[5] and to come into contact with one's true
and higher self, the divine Self.[6] Thus, the end goal of TM is contrary to the Christian end goal of meditation, which is union
with God.

TM claims numerous health benefits, but it is interwoven
with too many non-Christian beliefs and ideologies. Even TM
practices that focus on the physical health benefits still utilize
spiritual principles and practices contrary to Christ, which is
why Catholics should stay away from this practice. The Catholic
Church's document *Jesus Christ, the Bearer of the Water of Life*,
speaks to this:

> Many people are convinced that there is no harm in
> "borrowing" from the wisdom of the East, but the ex-
> ample of Transcendental Meditation (TM) should make
> Christians cautious about the prospect of committing
> themselves unknowingly to another religion (in this
> case, Hinduism), despite what TM's promoters claim
> about its religious neutrality. There is no problem with
> learning how to meditate, but the object or content of
> the exercise clearly determines whether it relates to the
> God revealed by Jesus Christ, to some other revelation,
> or simply to the hidden depths of the self.

The key principle is clear: TM is focused on the self and not on
Jesus Christ. Seeking to meditate and obtain peace of mind is
always encouraged for Christians, but it must be in a Christian
milieu. So, although TM may demonstrate some health benefits,
it still remains a practice that is incongruent with Jesus Christ
in much the same way Zen and Centering Prayer are. As Chris-

tians, we should not seek emptiness, connection to the self, or some divine enlightenment. We should seek only union with God (Father, Son, and Holy Spirit). God thinks of us constantly, so in prayer and meditation, he should be the sole focus of our attention in return.

Mindfulness

Many Westerners are always in a hurry and constantly busy. We rush around, trying to complete one thing after the next. We rarely finish the first task before thinking about accomplishing the next one. The trouble is that our to-do lists never end, and we spend our lives working, busy, and with our minds focused everywhere except on the present. Too many of us spend so much time *doing* and not enough time *being*, just enjoying life and focused on what really matters

Added to this are our addictions to cell phones, social media, Netflix, movies, video games, and so on. These things have created a culture of constant distraction and instant gratification. People find it increasingly difficult to sit quietly or to stay focused for even a short time.[7] In addition, more and more mental and emotional problems plague individuals. We spend so much time and energy regretting our past and fearing our future that many people struggle with worry and anxiety. Yet God is always found in the present moment. Until our feet stop running, our minds stop racing, and we learn to focus and be peaceful wherever we are, it will be extremely difficult to find God or to have an intimate relationship with him.

Many Christians are turning to mindfulness as a way to combat all of this. Their goal is to rein in out-of-control thoughts, conquer anxiety, and learn to be present. At its basic level, mindfulness is learning to live in and be aware of the present moment. Though it derives from Eastern religions, such as Hinduism and Buddhism, mindfulness has been developed as a strictly secular practice based on psychology. As we have noted elsewhere in this book, just because a practice derives from a non-Christian background does not necessarily mean that the practice itself is wrong and should be rejected, unless, of course, it is incompatible with our Catholic beliefs.

It is important to note that mindfulness is not like TM, Zen, or Centering Prayer. In other words, it is *not* prayer, meditation, or even a spiritual practice. It is also not a mind-emptying technique; rather, it is a neutral practice. There is nothing wrong with learning to live in the present moment and being aware of your thoughts and feelings and how you respond to them. In fact, Christians are called to do this. While Christians ultimately seek to find peace and contentment in God, sometimes other practices help us to grow, such as going to counseling, reading good self-help books, and mindfulness.

Brother Lawrence's spiritual classic *The Practice of the Presence of God* teaches Christians how to find God in the present moment and live in awareness of his presence. This is an important point. For Christians, the natural next step after learning to live in the present moment is to be aware of God, who dwells there. Our goal is to be aware of his presence in and around us at every moment, in whatever tasks we are undertaking.

Whether we are mowing the lawn, driving the car, taking a shower, going for a walk, or just sitting on the couch, we should be aware of God's presence. Unfortunately, our minds are often everywhere except where they should be. Yet God is found only in the present moment, and this is where we have to be if we want to encounter him. Thus, we need to learn to rein in our thoughts.

Dr. Gregory Bottaro, a Catholic clinical psychologist and founder of the CatholicPsych Institute, has written a book called *The Mindful Catholic*. This book (and his other work on the same subject) is based on the premise that God lives in the present moment, which is where we encounter him. Dr. Bottaro takes this neutral practice of mindfulness and places it in the context of a Catholic worldview. He says, "Learning how to practice mindfulness in a Catholic context is a way to recognize the dignity God created you with and take care of yourself accordingly."[8]

Although this mindfulness is not spiritual but psychological in nature, Bottaro designs his training within a Catholic framework to help Christians develop a better understanding of themselves, their lives, and ultimately, God. It also helps them to deal with psychological problems, such as anxiety, fear, and stress, which can hurt their relationship with God. Bottaro's exercises and practices help to calm and focus the mind in accordance with the Catholic Faith. If you are interested in learning more in this topic, I would refer you to Dr. Bottaro's books and his website, CatholicPsych.com.

Although mindfulness is not contrary to Catholic spirituality, there are some potential concerns to be aware of. First, it is important to be very clear that this practice is *not* prayer. In mindfulness sessions, a person is instructed to sit in silence once or twice a day for twenty minutes. This is meant to help focus the mind and deal with erratic thoughts, but it is not prayer and *not a substitute for prayer*, as Dr. Bottaro agrees. Mindfulness becomes a problem and a danger when it takes the place of prayer, especially in in our busy culture, in which it is a challenge to cultivate a deep prayer life if one is pressed for time.

The second concern is that some non-Catholic mindfulness, even though it is usually presented in a neutral way, can sometimes be placed in a context of New Age or Buddhist spirituality. Often, the practice is acceptable, but some teachers and promoters of the practice will add religious components to it or suggest follow-ups to mindfulness that are antithetical to our Catholic Faith. Moreover, mindfulness relaxes people, which can be a good thing, but that relaxed state also means that people may be more open and susceptible to those problematic teachings that some teachers may add on to the practice. Although mindfulness in itself does not pose a problem for Catholics, it is possible to become caught up in beliefs and ideologies that are non-Christian and even antithetical to our faith. For this reason, it is highly recommended that one practices mindfulness under the direction of orthodox Christians, such as Dr. Bottaro, who have made certain that there are no New Age beliefs or practices being peddled in addition to it. Anything in a mindfulness practice that goes against the Catholic Faith and the principles outlined in this book should be avoided.

Feng Shui

Imagine an episode from the TV show *Hoarders*. These people live with enormous piles of clutter, often stacked from floor to ceiling in every room of their house, leaving only enough space to walk from one room to the next. It is evident that their lives are out of balance and that something is blatantly wrong.

Now imagine a television show in which rich couples look at luxurious houses to buy. The homes are enormous, and every room is spotless. The yards have lush gardens, and every last inch is perfectly manicured. Flawlessly green shrubbery beckons the couples to come and stay in the extravagant paradise.

Given the choice, which of the two types of houses would you choose? Which would you feel more comfortable visiting? The obvious choice would be a beautiful house. One is a disastrous mess, and the other clean and ordered, which brings a certain sense of peace and security. This is the perspective from which Feng Shui flows. The goal of Feng Shui is to achieve peace and tranquility in life through the ordering of our houses and rooms. This involves placing everything, from furniture to décor, in a precise and symmetrical pattern that is designed to bring peace, balance, and tranquility of life.

Living clean, orderly lives and arranging our houses neatly is a good thing. The practice of Feng Shui, however, originates in Eastern spirituality that contains problematic beliefs and practices. Feng Shui practitioners endorse the Hindu worldview that everything is energy, and that life-force energy guides our lives. This energy flows in and around us at all moments, so rearranging the furniture in our homes can help to create straight pathways for the energy (chi) to flow. This is thought to enhance our life force and to allow the unique energy that is the divine Self to flow unobstructed. This practice also advocates the use of crystals to strengthen one's life-force energy. Crystals can "create a protective energy field" for the one who uses them.[9] Occasionally, some Feng Shui consultants even delve into I Ching, a Chinese form of magic and divination.

Bottom line: there is nothing wrong with keeping a tidy house and working to live in a tranquil atmosphere. For Christians, however, the practice of Feng Shui is problematic, as its ideologies are contrary to Christianity.

Crystals

Many people own crystals, from jewelry to chandelier attachments. Spiritualists place deep significance in the use of crystals, especially quartz crystals. In fact, although many quartz crystals are probably fine, many others may have evil spirits attached to them, as they are often sought after and used in occult practices. This is important for Christians to be aware of. Speaking from her experience, ex-New Age practitioner Moira Noonan warns: "Any crystals that you've ever been given or purchased — quartz crystals not lead crystal — you don't know whose hands they have passed through. They all have a history, and you don't know who has cut them or arranged them or handled them. Any crystal can be programmed. When it is programmed, a spirit is attached to it, and I don't mean the Holy Spirit. Demon spirits use crystals to enter your house. They are doorways. New Agers know that the first thing they have to do is clear their crystals."[10]

What does it mean to clear crystals? Karl Keating, founder of Catholic Answers, was once told not to touch specific crystals in a shop. After inquiring about the reason, Keating was told, "That would contaminate the stones. ... The stones pick up forces from anyone touching them, and contamination would have to be removed by 'clearing' the stones — by removing all the forces that have been built up in them."[11] This confirms what Noonan stated.

Of course, we are not suggesting that you throw away all of your jewelry, but just to be aware of crystals and their significance, especially in any problematic practices that may employ crystals, including Reiki, Feng Shui, certain massage therapies, and the like.

Acupuncture

Acupuncture is a technique derived from traditional Chinese medicine that attempts to heal patients by inserting needles in the skin at various energy points throughout the body. Similar to Reiki, Feng Shui, and other Eastern non-Christian practices, acupuncture is rooted in the belief that there is a universal life-force energy. It is said that this energy moves through pathways in the human body called meridians. Acupuncturists insert needles at certain points along the meridian line in order to remove energy blocks within a person and to help the energy to flow freely. The goal is to heal people physically or mentally and to help with any disorders they encounter.

The problem with acupuncture is that it's a spiritual practice derived from a non-Christian belief system. According to *Acupuncture Today*, "The vast majority of patients we see are imbalanced at the spirit level, regardless of the presence of physical symptoms. To truly and holistically heal, all levels must be addressed. To reach the spirit of a patient, we call upon the spirits of the points."[12] In other words, for acupuncture practitioners, the spiritual aspects of the practice are as important as (or more important than) the physical. These spiritual aspects are intertwined into this practice, including occult practices such as calling on the help of spirits. This can be done even without the patient's knowledge, which can be dangerous. Spiritual practices that work in the field of energy and chakras or call on spirits have potential for negative or even demonic activity. These are what we would term "doorways," and acupuncture can be a doorway. When practitioners call on spirits to heal people on a spiritual level, they are not invoking the Holy Spirit. For this reason alone, Christians should avoid this practice.

Apart from the spiritual aspects of acupuncture, the practice receives mixed reviews. Some patients swear by this practice, while others claim it does nothing. Medical and healthcare agencies say it's difficult to demonstrate that acupuncture works. Moreover, these agencies have disproved many false and fraudulent claims (including the claim to cure diabetes, Lyme disease, cancer, and other illnesses).[13] This is why Stephen Barrett, M.D., the head of a healthcare fraud watch, states that "acupuncture is an unproven modality of treatment. Its theory and practice are based on primitive and fanciful concepts of health and disease that bear no relationship to present scientific knowledge. Research during the past 20 years has not demonstrated that acupuncture is effective against any disease. Perceived effects of acupuncture are probably due to a combination of expectation, suggestion, counter-irritation, conditioning, and other psychologic mechanisms."[14]

In addition, "When not delivered properly, acupuncture can cause serious adverse effects, including infections, punctured organs, collapsed lungs, and injury to the central nervous system."[15]

Whether acupuncture works will continue to be debated, but this is not the issue for Christians. Acupuncture is a Chinese medicine developed from a false spiritual worldview that utilizes spiritual practices not in line with our Christian beliefs and possibly dangerous to our souls. Even if this practice were somehow void of spirituality, the amount of fraud and unscientific claims should make one keep away. Healthier alternatives to acupuncture include exercise, chiropractic care, massage, relaxation therapy, and even music, nature, and art therapy.

Yin and Yang

The Yin and Yang of Taoism reflects the belief that everything has an opposite, and these opposing, yet interdependent, forces work together to create a perfect balance. This belief traces its lineage back to I Ching, or Chinese divination. The Yin and

Yang is based on monism, universal energy, and other beliefs that come from the Chinese philosophy of Taoism. According to this belief, the two sides are two energies that blend together into a unified whole. In other words, there must be a balance in the universe, including equal amounts of good and evil, dark and light, positive and negative, male and female, and so on.

There are many problems with this worldview. Christians recognize evil as the absence of good, not a reality in its own right. And good certainly does not need to be balanced by evil. Even more troubling, proponents of Yin and Yang believe that this balance applies to everything in the universe, including God. Others assert that Satan is part of God and that his darkness and evil balance out God's light and goodness.[16] Moreover, the reality of this belief is that, "if opposites are always merging into and becoming each other, then there is no absolute good or evil."[17] These are just some of the many problems with the philosophical understanding of Yin and Yang. You may come across this symbol or teaching in certain martial arts, in some Chinese medicines, and even in Feng Shui.

Karma and Reincarnation

Karma states that we receive good or evil based on the decisions we make. Karma is a Hindu teaching that is connected to belief in reincarnation. Hindus explain, "The law of karma is a simple and straightforward concept according to which beings, not just men, are rewarded or punished according to their own actions and intentions. Thus, good actions and intentions reap good rewards and bad actions and intentions result in suffering and pain."[18]

According to this belief, those who live virtuously will move up the scale of karma, so to speak, and will enjoy a higher state of existence in their next life. Conversely, those who live evil lives will receive evil and suffering when they come back in their next life. According to the Hindu belief of karma and reincarnation, "A being has to live many lives and undergo many experiences before it attains perfection and becomes one with the Divine."[19] This is why this belief asserts that people are born again and again over millions of years until they eventually attain enlightenment and oneness with the divine being.[20] Other Eastern religions also accept reincarnation, as do many New Agers, though their beliefs on this vary.

Karma and reincarnation are irreconcilable with Christianity, and they do not hold up to logic or Christian spirituality. For example, Jesus Christ lived a perfect life. He healed people, forgave sins, performed countless good deeds, and loved everyone, including those who hated him. Yet, despite all of this, Jesus suffered one of the most gruesome deaths in history. Did he deserve that? Did he attract it to himself through his deeds? The same might be asked of Martin Luther King Jr., the African-American preacher who fought for civil rights, preached peace and love, and worked tirelessly for the good of mankind. He was killed in cold blood, which is completely contrary to karma.

The obvious answer is that karma is not true, and neither Jesus nor Dr. King attracted by their actions the evils they suffered. Moreover, it is also impossible for a Catholic, or for any Christian, to accept reincarnation. Although it is true that we will be rewarded for our good deeds and punished for evil ones (Rv 20:12–13), the Bible specifically teaches that each of us will face judgment immediately after death. From there, heaven (perhaps by way of purgatory) or hell will be our eternal destiny. Thus, we do not come back again and again, but we die once and then meet God (Heb 9:27). The Catholic Church teaches, "Both cosmic unity and reincarnation are irreconcilable with the Christian belief; a human person is a distinct being, who lives one life, for which he or she is fully responsible."[21]

In the Christian worldview, each human person is given one chance and all the knowledge he or she needs to choose God or reject him. Therefore, a Christian must depend wholly on Jesus, who is the only way to heaven (Acts 4:12). Christian theology teaches that sin created a debt that we cannot pay back on our own. It has established an infinite canyon between us and God, which we cannot cross ourselves. For this reason, the Son of God became man for our sake. Jesus took the punishment that was due to us when he died on the cross to wash away sin. Because he shed his blood for our sins, we can find forgiveness, freedom, and salvation if we repent and follow Jesus, no matter how much evil we may have done in our lives.

Past Life Regression

Past-life-regression (PLR) therapy, which is based on reincarnation, claims to bring spiritual and emotional healing to people's lives. PLR therapists use hypnosis allegedly to lead patients back in time to earlier memories and even to supposed past lives. PLR practitioners contend that one may experience a glimpse of his previous life or encounter it in great detail; this could include anything from viewing himself as a baby to witnessing how he died in his former life.

In PLR, a trained guide (or facilitator) claims to help patients to see particular circumstances from their past lives that have caused their current problems in this life. The goal is to learn to release negative blocks that are holding patients back from being free.

Carol Bowman, a PLR practitioner with thirty years of experience in the field, explains, "Past life regression is a therapeutic technique for accessing and re-experiencing your past lives directly. ... Negative patterns fuel destructive, compulsive behavior, cloud judgment, cause injury, and block your way. By making these memories conscious, we can release the patterns that no longer serve us, freeing us to live more fully in the present."[22] On her website, Bowman explains that the treatment involves hypnotization, but that patients are only in "a light trance."[23]

Moria Noonan, a former PLR therapist, was deeply involved in the practice. In her book *Ransomed from Darkness*, she informs her readers, "Regression therapies are only meaningful if one believes in reincarnation, a belief that is fundamental to New Age thinking. ... Indeed, in any system where a person functions as his own savior, more than one lifetime would certainly be required. I know now that the past life experiences I once induced were either imaginary or were drawn from experiences earlier in a client's present life."[24]

Like so many of these spiritual and alternative therapies, many mental health and fraud agencies have rebuked this practice as scientifically unfounded, fraudulent, and even unethical. [25] According to the *Journal of Medical Ethics and History of Medicine*, "It is unethical to propose to a patient to go back to a previous life to come to terms with a traumatic event in order to treat a phobia, when in fact, it is much more efficient to do so through some of the techniques in behavioral therapy. ... Furthermore, the time and resources wasted on past life regression could be better allocated to therapies that are far more efficient, especially in the treatment of phobias."[26]

PLR is not only a waste of time and money, but its worldview is steeped in reincarnation and other philosophical ideas that do not mesh with Christian beliefs. Like many of these New Age practices, there is no way that PLR could help Christians, as it requires entering into a milieu that goes directly against God. Therefore, Christians should find healing in viable, trustworthy ways.

Shamanism

Shamanism is a religion of spiritualism practiced by ancient indigenous people of far Northern Europe and Siberia. It centers on a Shaman, who is considered the spiritual leader of a tribe or culture. "The word shaman comes from Siberia and means 'one who sees in the dark' (the hidden realities), and widely refers to those who are medicine women/men, healers, and seers."[27] The Merriam-Webster dictionary defines "shaman" as "a priest or priestess who uses magic for the purpose of curing the sick, divining the hidden, and controlling events."[28]

One shamanic site describes how this spiritual practice works: "A shaman works to restore balance and wholeness by addressing the root cause of the problem. Many methods are used in shamanic healing, including soul retrieval, retrieval of a spiritual ally, removal of unwanted energies, soul remembering, ancestral work, psychopomp (helping the deceased to cross over into the Light) and hands on healing."[29]

It should be clear that shamanism is a dark practice of magic that is steeped in occultic spiritualism and divination. A shaman enters into a trance, or an altered state of consciousness, to perform many of his works, and the spirits he calls upon may take the form of animals, which is known as shape-shifting. It is also believed that shamans can turn themselves into animals.[30]

There are different types of shamans, ranging from spiritual leaders and healers of indigenous peoples to a more modern conception of New Age esoteric gurus. Although these people may be sincere, the powers they are meddling with do not come from God. Therefore, anything connected to a shaman or shamanism is spiritually dangerous and could easily be a doorway to the dark side or even demonic possession. Consequently, Christians should stay far away from anything related to shamanism.

Alex and Ani

Alex and Ani is a popular line of jewelry. Their famous bracelets include an extensive range of choices, from the Eye of Horus to medals of saints. The problem with Alex and Ani is that their products are not just jewelry. They are steeped in New Age and occult spirituality, and the company advertises that each piece of jewelry is infused with the energy of the universe.

The *New York Times* featured the company in a 2014 story. "Do you want 'limitless power, limitless good karma, and limitless wisdom'? Alex and Ani's promotional material tells you to buy the Buddha Charm Bangle, available for $28. Do you want 'divine direction and soulful enlightenment'? They recommend the Saint Anthony Charm Bangle, for the same price. For the union of masculine and feminine energy, Alex and Ani offers the Star of David Charm Bangle, at $24."[31]

These marketing materials make clear the company's anti-Christian and spiritually problematic ideology. Yet the business is confusing for Catholics, because Alex and Ani sells Catholic religious goods, including Miraculous Medals and saint medals, such as the Saint Anthony medal mentioned above. Be warned! These medals are not Catholic. Whereas Catholic medals are blessed by priests, each piece of jewelry sold by Alex and Ani is infused with energy and prayed over and blessed by shamans. The owner of the shop told the *Times*, "Before they are sold in the store, 'every product has been blessed by my priests, it has been blessed by my shaman friends, protected from radio frequency, from radioactivity.' "[32]

As discussed in our last section, shamanism is a demonic practice of magic and sorcery, and for Alex and Ani to dabble in New Age and occult spirituality is dangerous. A friend of mine told me a story about an exorcist who walked past a woman who was wearing an Alex and Ani bracelet. The exorcist had never met this woman, but he stopped dead in his tracks as he walked by her. The priest asked her where she had bought her bracelet. "Alex and Ani," she replied. "Take it off: it's cursed!" urged the exorcist. The woman was shocked. She told the priest the medal was the Blessed Virgin Mary. The exorcist insisted, "Well, take it off: it's cursed!" Remember, spirits are real — and the only good spirit is the Holy Spirit. If any object has been "blessed" in the name of any other spirit, it is dangerous. As Christians, we must avoid these objects.

If you have purchased religious jewelry from Alex and Ani,

it is strongly recommended that you throw it away and have nothing further to do with it. You can find religious jewelry and medals in trustworthy stores, and you do not need to patronize this business, as its New Age spirituality impacts everything they sell, including apparently Catholic items. Of course, this company is trying to do good, but nothing good can come from jewelry that is prayed over and blessed by shamans. If the Devil is attached to an object through blessings and prayers to false gods, then that item could be a doorway to the demonic.

* * *

In this chapter, we have discussed some of the more popular spiritual practices that Christians may encounter and how they can be dangerous for our souls. This information is not only to inform you on these issues but also to help you form your conscience in line with Church teaching in these matters. Of course, neither this chapter nor this book is exhaustive. Rather, it is meant to provide the tools to help you spiritually discern any beliefs or questionable practices you may encounter in the future.

FINAL THOUGHTS

L ife is too short to allow yourself to be deceived by counter-feit spirituality. Cardinal Timothy Dolan, archbishop of New York, remarked, "Maybe the greatest threat to the Church is not heresy, not dissent, not secularism, not even moral relativism, but this sanitized, feel-good, boutique, therapeutic spiritual-ity that makes no demands, calls for no sacrifice, asks for no conversion, entails no battle against sin, but only soothes and affirms."[1] Dolan astutely identifies one of the chief problems with false spirituality: it is a completely subjective spirituality, in which we decide what is right and wrong and what we wish to believe.

There is no doubt that the road to heaven is difficult. Jesus taught us that. But it is worth it — eternally! In a dark, often immoral culture, and in a world where people are starving for the truth, Jesus Christ is the resplendent Light of the world. In a time of scandal, corruption, and spiritual disease, even in the Church, we need to pray and develop an even deeper relation-ship with Christ. We must also trust and remain close to the Catholic Church, which Jesus founded and which the Holy Spir-it guides into all truth.

Throughout the more than 2,000 years of her existence, the Catholic Church has been a light in the darkness. The Church has been the largest charity in the world, feeding, clothing, and educating more people than any other institution has. The Cath-olic Church started hospitals and orphanages, created the uni-versity system,[2] invented economics and the scientific method, and advanced science and mathematics perhaps more than most organizations on earth have.

This same Church chose the books of the Bible under the inspiration of the Holy Spirit and put the Bible together under one cover as we know it today. Catholic monks copied the Holy Scriptures day by day, line by line, letter by letter for over a thousand years, until the printing press was invented, so we could always have the Word of God. Throughout the "Dark Ages," the Catholic Church shone as a bright light. The Church civilized the Vikings and the many barbarian tribes that pillaged the Roman Empire for hundreds of years. The Church has also produced some of the best architecture, music, and art in history. This is only a smattering of what the Catholic Church has done out of love for Jesus and his creation.

There will always be some bad eggs in the Church, and in any organization; even Jesus foretold that. But he also promised that he would be present with his Church, guiding her until the end of time. Let us then trust in Jesus, the Way, the Truth, and the Life. In dark times, when evil attacks and threatens to destroy our Church, and phony spiritualities sprout up in the culture at large and even within Catholic organizations, let us remember that the truth has already been established by Christ. Let us not forget that Jesus is always Lord, and he is always seated on the throne. Likewise, let us remember that the Church is the beautiful Bride of Christ, and we cannot have Christ without his Church, the same Church of which he promised: "the gates of Hades shall not prevail against it" (Mt 16:18).

Also call to mind the many holy and heroic saints who rose up in dark times, in different places across the world, and took on various difficulties that bombarded the Church. They challenged people in a humble yet powerful way. They inspired generations through the holiness of their lives, and they changed the world around them through the power of God. When times became rough, they prayed, fasted, and lived virtuously. Remember, *saints make other saints*, and saints change the world!

If you would like to change the world in some way, and if you wish to inspire people to follow the truth, then strive for sainthood — to become everything Jesus Christ created you to be. This can be accomplished only by remaining on the straight and narrow way, and by fostering a deep, personal relationship with Jesus Christ. Do not let anyone convince you that there is another faster, easier, or more impressive way to eternal life. Jesus Christ is the Way, and as Christians, we know he is the only way to eternal life.

Where Do We Go from Here?

Perhaps some of your family, friends, coworkers, or other loved ones are ensnared in some sort of false spirituality, and you do not know how to reach them. Below are some practical tips for sharing the truth and making a difference in the lives of those trapped in counterfeit spiritualities.

1. *Pray.* It is imperative to cultivate and foster your own deep prayer life. In general, there is always some aspect of spiritualism (to varying degrees) attached to any false practice that people are entangled in. This often blinds those involved, so they cannot recognize the truth. Attempting to discuss or reason with them often proves fruitless. Usually their arguments and defenses are emotional and subjective rather than rational and objective. This is why prayer is absolutely important. We must pray often that God will have mercy on them, give sight to their blindness, and help free them from the chains that bind them. Pray!

2. *Love them.* It is important always to love these people with a great love, even while rejecting the practices they are involved in. We must model the love, joy, and peace of Christ, praying that his light will draw them back to the truth. We need to treat them

lovingly, even when it is difficult. Sometimes it is easy to demonize the *person* instead of the *action*, which only alienates the person from us and from the truth we are trying to share. Although we cannot accept others' errors or false rationales, we need to let them know that we are always there for them unconditionally.

Sometimes this takes the form of friendly dialogue and discussion about these matters. At other times, it means having normal conversations about life, work, and other subjects that have nothing to do with spirituality. It is crucial that we be genuinely interested in the lives of people we know who are caught up in counterfeit spiritualities and that we earn their trust by showing that interest. If they ever decide to return to truth, are we the kinds of people they can trust and approach? Or do we push people away and make enemies by our words and actions? There is a fine line between helping people to see the error of their ways and judging them, looking down on them, or being cynical and critical toward them. Love the person, hate the sin.

3. *Study.* Don't stop after reading this book. Now that you know what to look out for, continue to read and learn about these issues from faithful sources. In addition, commit to learning as much as you can about your Catholic Faith. The more you study, the more you will be able to help others, and the less likely it will be for you to be led astray. This can be accomplished by reading good Catholic books (see the bibliography and appendix for recommended reading), visiting Catholic websites, taking orthodox Catholic courses, and listening to or watching podcasts or YouTube videos that are faithful to Catholic teachings.

4. *Invite people back.* People who are involved in a New
   Age or esoteric spirituality are usually sincerely
   seeking fulfillment. Many of these people have good
   hearts and have unknowingly been misled. Even if
   you know people who have freely (and perhaps even
   knowingly) chosen to embrace these counterfeit spiritualities, periodically invite them back to church, or
   to a prayer meeting, a Bible study, Eucharistic ado-
   ration, or some other event or activity. Alternately,
   share with them good literature and resources that
   might help them see and embrace the truth. If they
   accept what you have to say, then you have won them
   over. If they reject you, continue to pray for them.

My prayer is that you found this book helpful, enlightening, in-
formative, and inspiring. I pray that you will be motivated to
share this message with others and to help shine the light of
heaven into the darkness. May God's infinite and holy light of
truth shatter the surrounding darkness of night, and may he fill
us with the love and the very life of his Son, the risen Lord Jesus
Christ!

Know the truth. It will set you free (Jn 8:32).

APPENDIX
Continued Learning

Audio

Oprah: Televangelist of the New Age Deception, by Sharon Lee Giganti (Catholic Answers, 2007).

Overcoming the New Age Movement, by Matthew Arnold (St. Joseph Communications, 2018).

Former Satanist Becomes Catholic, by Betty Brennan (The Augustine Institute, 2019).

What Is New Age? by Moira Noonan (Moiranoonan.org).

Relevant Websites

www.NewAgeDeception.com

www.ChristianAnswersForTheNewAge.org

www.Catholic.com

www.EWTN.com

Relevant Church Documents

Congregation for the Doctrine of Faith, "Declaration *Dominus Iesus* on the Unicity and Salvific Universality of Jesus Christ and the Church," August 6, 2000, vatican.va.

Benedict XVI, "Letter to the Bishops of the Catholic Church on Some Aspects of Christian Meditation," October 15, 1989, vatican.va.

Congregation for the Doctrine of the Faith, "On Some Aspects of Christian Meditation," October 15, 1989, vatican.va.

USCCB Committee on Doctrine, "Guidelines for Evaluating Reiki as an Alternative Therapy," 2009.

Pontifical Council for Culture and Pontifical Council for Interreligious Dialogue, *Jesus Christ, the Bearer of the Water of Life: A Christian Reflection on the "New Age,"* vatican.va.

The Catechism of the Catholic Church, digital format available at vatican.va and usccb.org.

Books
Books on New Age Spirituality

Johnnette S. Benkovic, *The New Age Counterfeit: A Study Guide for Individual or Group Use* (Faith Pub Co.; revised edition, 1997).

Reverend James J. LeBar, *Cults, Sects, and the New Age* (Huntington, IN: Our Sunday Visitor, 1989).

Moira Noonan, *Ransomed from Darkness: The New Age, Christian Faith and the Battle for Souls* (El Sobrante, CA: North Bay Books, 2005).

Father Mitch Pacwa, S.J., *Catholics and the New Age: How Good People Are Being Drawn into Jungian Psychology, the Enneagram, and the Age of Aquarius* (Ann Arbor, MI: Servant, 1992).

Ralph Rath, *The New Age: A Christian Critique* (South Bend, IN: Greenlawn Press, 1990).

Catholic Spirituality and Inspiration

Father Gabriele Amorth, *An Exorcist Tells His Story* (San Francisco: Ignatius Press, 1999).

Raymond Arroyo, *Mother Angelica: The Story of a Nun, Her Nerve, and a Network of Miracles* (New York: Doubleday, 2005).

Matt Baglio, *The Rite: The Making of a Modern Exorcist* (New York: Doubleday, 2009).

Father Donald H. Calloway, MIC, *No Turning Back: A Witness to Mercy* (Stockbridge, MA: Marian Press, 2010).

Joan Carroll Cruz, *Eucharistic Miracles and Eucharistic Phenomena in the Lives of the Saints* (Charlotte, NC: TAN Books, 2010).

Joan Carroll Cruz, *The Incorruptibles: A Study of the Incorruption of the Bodies of Various Catholic Saints and Beati* (Charlotte, NC: TAN Books, 2012).

Saint Francis de Sales, *Introduction to the Devout Life.*

Jean C. J. d'Elbée, *I Believe in Love: A Personal Retreat Based on the Teaching of St. Thérèse of Lisieux* (Manchester, NH: Sophia Institute Press, 2001).

Thomas Dubay, SM, *Prayer Primer: Igniting a Fire Within* (San Francisco: Ignatius Press, 2002).

Thomas Dubay, SM, *Fire Within: St. Teresa of Avila, St. John of the Cross and the Gospel — On Prayer* (San Francisco: Ignatius Press, 1989).

Scott Hahn, *The Lamb's Supper: The Mass as Heaven on Earth* (New York: Doubleday, 1999).

Scott and Kimberly Hahn, *Rome Sweet Home: Our Journey to Catholicism* (San Francisco: Ignatius Press, 1993).

Saint Ignatius of Loyola, *Spiritual Exercises.*

Matthew Kelly, *Rediscover Jesus: An Invitation* (n.p.: Beacon Publishing, 2015).

Matthew Kelly, *Resisting Happiness* (n.p.: Beacon Publishing, 2016).

Thomas á Kempis, *The Imitation of Christ.*

Brother Lawrence, *The Practice of the Presence of God.*

Sister Briege McKenna, OSC, *Miracles Do Happen: God Can Do the Impossible* (Ann Arbor, MI: Servant, 2002).

Thomas E. Woods, *How the Catholic Church Built Western Civilization* (Washington, DC: Regnery, 2005).

Beginner Books on God and the Catholic Faith
Dr. John Bergsma, *Bible Basics for Catholics: A New Picture of Salvation History* (Notre Dame, IN: Ave Maria Press, 2012).

Matthew Kelly, *Rediscover Catholicism: A Spiritual Guide to Living with Passion and Purpose* (n.p.: Beacon Publishing, 2010).

Bryan Mercier, *WHY Do You Believe in God?: Catholic Conversations with Skeptics and Non-Believers* (self-pub., CreateSpace Independent Publishing, 2016).

Matthew Pinto, *Did Jesus Have a Last Name? And 199 Other Questions from Catholic Teenagers* (West Chester, PA: Ascension Press, 2005).

Matthew Pinto, *Did Adam and Eve Have Belly Buttons? And 199 Other Questions from Catholic Teenagers* (West Chester, PA: Ascension Press, 1998).

Brant Pitre, *The Case for Jesus: The Biblical and Historical Evidence for Christ* (New York: Image, 2016).

Reverend Peter M. J. Stravinskas, Catholic Answer Book Series (Huntington, IN: Our Sunday Visitor, 1990–2003).

Father John Trigilio Jr. and Father Kenneth Brighenti, *Catholicism for Dummies* (Hoboken, NJ: Wiley, 2012).

Books to Help You Go Deeper in Your Faith
Dave Armstrong, *A Biblical Defense of Catholicism* (Manchester, NH: Sophia Institute Press, 2003).

Pope Emeritus Benedict XVI, *A School of Prayer* (San Francisco: Ignatius Press, 2013).

Thomas Dubay, SM, *Fire Within: St. Teresa of Avila, St. John of the Cross and the Gospel — On Prayer* (San Francisco: Ignatius Press, 1989).

Thomas Dubay, SM, *Prayer Primer: Igniting a Fire Within* (San Francisco, CA: Ignatius Press, 2002).

Saint Francis de Sales, *Introduction to the Devout Life.*

Saint Ignatius of Loyola, *The Spiritual Exercises.*

Karl Keating, *Catholicism and Fundamentalism: The Attack on "Romanism" by "Bible Christians"* (San Francisco: Ignatius Press, 1988).

Peter J. Kreeft and Ronald Tacelli, *Handbook of Catholic Apologetics: Reasoned Answers to Questions of Faith* (San Francisco: Ignatius Press, 2009).

Brother Lawrence, *The Practice of the Presence of God.*

Patrick Madrid, *Pope Fiction: Answers to 30 Myths and Misconceptions about the Papacy* (Rancho Santa Fe, CA: Basilica Press, 1999).

Patrick Madrid, *Search and Rescue: How to Bring Your Family and Friends into — or Back into — the Catholic Church* (Manchester, NH: Sophia Institute Press, 2012).

Frank Sheed, *Theology for Beginners* (Brooklyn, NY: Angelico Press, 2011).

Frank Sheed, *Theology and Sanity* (London: Aeterna Press, 2019).

Acknowledgments

I would first like to thank my wife, Katherine, who continually supports me, my ministry, and my mission. I would also like to acknowledge Carrie O'Connell in a special way. Her help was invaluable, and without her, this book may not have been possible. Lastly, I would like to send a special thank-you to Katie de le Reyes and Stephanie Villeda, who were incredibly helpful, and to all who assisted in some way with this book. THANK YOU!

NOTES

PREFACE

1. Tim Challies, "Counterfeit Detection (Part 1)," Challies, June 27, 2006, accessed August 18, 2019, https://www.challies.com /articles/counterfeit-detection-part-1/.

2. Donna Steichen, *Ungodly Rage: The Hidden Face of Catholic Feminism* (San Francisco: Ignatius Press, 1991), 23.

CHAPTER 1

1. Congregation for the Doctrine of Faith, "Notification on the book *Toward a Christian Theology of Religious Pluralism* by Father Jacques Dupuis, S.J.," Vatican website, January 24, 2001, accessed November 8, 2018, http://www.vatican.va /roman_curia/congregations/cfaith/documents/rc_con_cfaith_ doc_20010124_dupuis_en.html.

CHAPTER 2

1. Rhonda Byrne, *The Secret* (New York: Atria Books, 2006), 162.

2. Eckhart Tolle, *The Power of NOW: A Guide to Spiritual Enlightenment* (Novato, CA: New World Library, 1999), 15.

3. Ibid., 9. See also Deepak Chopra, *The Third Jesus: The Christ We Cannot Ignore* (New York: Three Rivers Press, 2008), 104.

4. Byrne, *The Secret*, 164.

5. Marianne Williamson, *The Gift of Change: Spiritual Guidance for Living Your Best Life* (New York: HarperCollins, 2004), 94, 105.

6. Tolle, *The Power of NOW*, 104.

7. This concept of true Self and false self is popular in New Age spiritual books and even in many fraudulent Catholic ones. Sister Joyce Rupp and Father M. Basil Pennington (d. 2005), as just two examples, have promoted this line of thinking. Father Pennington penned a book titled *True Self, False Self*.

8. Helen Schucman, *A Course in Miracles: Combined Volume*, 2nd ed. (New York: Penguin Group, 1996), lessons 93 and 95 in workbook.

9. Dr. Wayne W. Dyer, *Your Sacred Self* (New York: HarperCollins, 1995), 12, 350–51.

10. Thomas Keating, *Open Mind, Open Heart*, 20th-anniversary ed. (New York: Continuum International, 2006), 158.

Chapter 3

1. Neale Donald Walsch, *Conversations with God: An Uncommon Dialogue*, vol. 2 (Charlottesville, VA: Hampton Roads Publishing, 1997), 42.

2. Byrne, *The Secret*, 4, 7.

3. Ibid., 68, 160.

4. Ibid., 139.

5. Walsch, *Conversations: An Uncommon Dialogue*, vol. 1 (New York: G. P. Putnam's Sons, 1995), 105–6.

6. Vicky Thompson, *The Jesus Path: 7 Steps to a Cosmic Awakening* (Boston: Red Wheel/Weiser, 2003), 32–34; James J. Lebar, *Cults, Sects, and the New Age Movement* (Huntington, IN: Our Sunday Visitor, 1989), 160–61; Byrne, *The Secret*, 47.

7. Sharon Lee Giganti, *Oprah: Televangelist of the New Age Deception* (San Diego: Catholic Answers, 2007), CD-ROM.

Chapter 4

1. Fr. Gabriele Amorth, *An Exorcist: More Stories* (San Francisco: Ignatius Press, 2002), 114.

2. See also Lv 19:31; Is 47:12–15; Jer 10:1–3; Acts 16:16–18, 19:18.

3. "As Above, So Below," Astrology for Aquarius, accessed July 28, 2019, https://astrologyforaquarius.com/articles/363/as-above-so-below.

4. Parke Krunkle, "Sign of the Times: Astrology Story Soars Like a Comet," *Star Tribune*, January 14, 2011, accessed September 30, 2018, http://www.startribune.com/sign-of-the-times-astrology-story-soars-like-a-comet/113100139/.

5. Pedro Braganca, "Astrology: Why Your Zodiac Sign and Horoscope Are Wrong," *Live Science*, September 21, 2017, accessed September 23, 2019, https://www.livescience.com/4667-astrological-sign.html.

6. Phil Plait, "No, NASA Hasn't Changed the Zodiac Signs or Added a New One," *New Scientist*, September 27, 2016, accessed September 23, 2019, https://www.newscientist.com/article/2107207-no-nasa-hasnt-changed-the-zodiac-signs-or-added-a-new-one/.

7. Ashley Hamer, "Astrology Might Be Fun, but It Sure Isn't Science," *Curiosity Makes You Smarter*, January 27, 2017, accessed September 23, 2019, https://curiosity.com/topics/astrology-might-be-fun-but-it-sure-isnt-science-curiosity/.

8. Ralph Rath, *The New Age: A Christian Critique* (South Bend, IN: Greenlawn Press, 1990), 71.

9. Matthew Arnold, *Overcoming the New Age Movement* (Sycamore, IL: Catholic Lighthouse Media, 2008), CD-ROM.

10. Father Mitch Pacwa, SJ, *Catholics and the New Age* (Ann Arbor, MI: Servant, 1992), 89.

11. David Moye, "Sylvia Browne: Dead Psychic's Legacy Riddled with Failed Predictions, Fraud," *Huffington Post*, November 21, 2013, accessed September 23, 2019, https://www.huffingtonpost.com/2013/11/21/sylvia-browne_n_4317470.html.

12. Ibid.

13. Michael Shermer, "Psychic for a Day: How I Learned Tarot Cards, Palm Reading, Astrology, and Mediumship in 24 Hours," *Skeptic Magazine* 10, no. 1 (2003), https://www.quackwatch.org/01QuackeryRelatedTopics/psychic2.html.

14. Michael Wilson, "Seeing Freedom in Their Future, Psychics Reveal All: 'It's a Scam, Sir,'" *New York Times*, August 28, 2015, https://www.nytimes.com/2015/08/29/nyregion/the-secret -to-the-psychic-trade-its-in-the-parole-board-transcripts.html. Stephen Barrett, MD, "Sylvia Browne: Psychic or Con Artist?" Quackwatch, December 14, 2013, accessed September 23, 2019, https://www.quackwatch.org/11Ind/browne.html.

15. Arnold, *Overcoming the New Age Movement.*

16. Ibid.

17. Marcia Montenegro, "Should Christians Read Horoscopes?," *Reasons for Jesus*, August 13, 2017, accessed September 23, 2019, http://reasonsforjesus.com/should-christians-read-horoscopes/.

18. Gabriele Amorth, *An Exorcist Tells His Story* (San Francisco: Ignatius Press, 1999), 112.

19. Moira Noonan, *Ransomed from Darkness* (El Sobrante, CA: North Bay Books, 2005), 45–46.

20. Amorth, *An Exorcist Tells His Story*, 30.

21. Ibid., 149.

22. Arnold, *Overcoming the New Age Movement.*

CHAPTER 5

1. Mark Singleton, *Yoga Body: The Origins of Modern Posture Practice* (New York: Oxford University Press, 2010), 26.

2. Rosen, Richard, *Yoga FAQ* (Boulder: Shambahla Publications, 2017), 24.

3. The earliest known texts on yoga include the Vedas, the Upanishads, the *Bhagavad Gita*, and the *Yoga Sutras*.

4. Russill Paul, *Jesus in the Lotus: The Mystical Doorway between Christianity and Yogic Spirituality* (Novato, CA: New World Library, 2009), 9.

5. The *Encyclopedia Britannica* says that *samadhi* is the "Highest state of mental concentration that a person can achieve while still bound to the body and which unites him with the highest reality. *Samadhi* is a state of profound and utterly absorptive contemplation of the Absolute that is undisturbed by

desire, anger, or any other ego-generated thought or emotion. It is a state of joyful calm, or even of rapture and beatitude, in which one maintains one's full mental alertness and acuity. *Samadhi* is regarded in Hinduism and Buddhism as the climax of all spiritual and intellectual activity. The power to attain *samadhi* is a precondition of attaining release from the cycle of death and rebirth." "Samadhi," in *Encyclopedia Britannica*, accessed September 25, 2019, https://www.britannica.com /topic/samadhi-Indian-philosophy.

6. Swami Jnaneshvara Bharati, "*Modern* Yoga vs. *Traditional* Yoga," Swamij.com, accessed September 25, 2019, http://www .swamij.com/traditional-yoga.htm.

7. B. K. S. Iyengar, *Light on Yoga* (New York: Schocken Books, 1976), 21–22.

8. Being a Christian organization, the YMCA was one of the first groups to have a mind-body-spirit connection in its physical practice, something not heard of in yoga at this time. This connection, cultivated by the YMCA and other organizations, such as the Swedish gymnastics, would later influence the people of India and their practice of yoga in the great fitness revival, during which they were ministered to and taught by the YMCA. Singleton, *Yoga Body*, 84–85.

9. Singleton, *Yoga Body*, 22, 33, 81–86.

10. Mark Singleton, "The Ancient and Modern Roots of Yoga," *Yoga Journal*, April 16, 2018, accessed September 25, 2019, https://www.yogajournal.com/yoga-101/yoga-s-greater-truth.

11. Singleton, *Yoga Body*, 145.

12. Ibid., 114–115, 33. Singleton details how Europe brought a physical culture to India and trained them in it. Over time, the Indians eventually adapted these physical practices for their own purposes and incorporated them into their own tradition of yoga.

13. Russill Paul, *Jesus in the Lotus*, 111–12.

14. Iyengar, *Yoga*, 32–33, 36.

15. Rosen, *Yoga FAQ*, 146.

16. Paul, *Jesus in the Lotus*, 111–12.

17. Amorth, *An Exorcist Tells His Story*, 54.

18. "Our Position on Yoga," Pietra Fitness, accessed September 25, 2019, https://pietrafitness.com/pf-not-yoga/.

19. WholyFit.com, accessed September 25, 2019.

20. "Nimbus," *Catholic Encyclopedia*, accessed September 25, 2019, http://www.newadvent.org/cathen/11080b.htm.

CHAPTER 6

1. Walter Lübeck, Frank Arjava Petter, and William Lee Rand, *The Spirit of Reiki: The Complete Handbook of the Reiki System* (Twin Lakes, WI: Lotus Press, 2003), 13–15.

2. Ibid., 16–17.

3. Ibid., 21–22.

4. The International Center for Reiki Training, "How Does Reiki Work?," Reiki.org, accessed September 25, 2019, http://www.reiki.org/faq/howdoesreikiwork.html.

5. Susan Brinkmann, *Learn to Discern: Is It Christian or New Age? Energy Medicine* (Oldsmar, FL: Simon Peter Press, 2008), 19.

6. Lübeck et al., *The Spirit of Reiki*, 61–62.

7. Ibid., 75–76.

8. "Energy Medicine: An Overview," Healthy, accessed September 25, 2019, https://healthy.net/2005/07/01/energy-medicine-an-overview/.

9. "What Is Energy Medicine?," Foundation for the Advancement of Energy Medicine, Inc., accessed September 25, 2019, http://faemt.org, emphasis added.

10. "Reiki: In Depth," National Center for Complementary and Integrative Health, accessed December 15, 2019, https://nccih.nih.gov/sites/nccam.nih.gov/files/Reiki_11-30-2015.pdf.

11. Tim Newman, "Everything You Need to Know about Reiki," *Medical News Today*, September 6, 2017, accessed September 25, 2019, https://www.medicalnewstoday.com/articles/308772.php.

12. William T. Jarvis, Ph.D., "Reiki," National Council against Health Fraud, December 1, 2000, accessed September 25, 2019, https://www.ncahf.org/articles/o-r/reiki.html.

13. "JREF Results," James Randi Educational Foundation, accessed September 25, 2019, https://web.randi.org/home /jref-status.

14. For example, William Rand of the International Center for Reiki Training, one of the foremost authorities on Reiki, posits similarities between Jesus' ministry and Reiki: "There are many similarities between the laying on of hands healing Jesus did and the practice of Reiki. One important similarity is the fact that Jesus could pass the power to heal on to others which is similar to the Reiki attunement process. ... The fact that Jesus had secret teachings he gave only to those who he had given healing power is clearly indicated in Matthew 13:10–11 and Mark 4:10–12 & 34. Secret knowledge is also part of the Reiki teachings in that the symbols as well as the process of doing attunements are traditionally kept secret and only made available to those who take a Reiki class." William Lee Rand, "Similarities between the Healing of Jesus and Reiki," International Center for Reiki Training, accessed September 25, 2019, http:// www.reiki.org/reikinews/reikin16.html.

15. M. J. Farabee, "Laws of Thermodynamics," Estrella Mountain Community College, accessed September 25, 2019, https:// www2.estrellamountain.edu/faculty/farabee/biobk /BioBookEner1.html.

16. Patrick Olivelle, "Upanishad," *Encyclopedia Britannica*, accessed September 25, 2019, https://www.britannica.com/topic /Upanishad.

17. "Shakti," *New World Encyclopedia*, accessed September 26, 2019, https://www.newworldencyclopedia.org/entry/Shakti.

18. See Mt 10:28; Mk 8:36–37, 12:30.

19. Elizabeth Palermo, "What Is Reiki?," *Live Science*, February 19, 2015, accessed September 26, 2019, https://www.livescience. com/40275-reiki.html. See also Stephen Barrett, M.D., "Reiki Is

Nonsense," Quackwatch, accessed September 26, 2019, https://www.quackwatch.org/01QuackeryRelatedTopics/reiki.html.

20. A. Catlin and R. L. Taylor-Ford, "Investigation of Standard Care versus Sham Reiki Placebo versus Actual Reiki Therapy to Enhance Comfort and Well-Being in a Chemotherapy Infusion Center," National Center for Biotechnology Information, accessed September 26, 2019, https://www.ncbi.nlm.nih.gov/pubmed/21531671.

21. Ibid.

22. Briege McKenna, *Miracles Do Happen* (New York: St. Martin Press, 1987), 24.

23. Brinkmann, *Energy Medicine*, 26–27. The *Catechism of the Catholic Church* confirms the correct nature of healing in paragraph 699.

24. Amorth, *An Exorcist Tells His Story*, 160. It is also important to note that even when there appear to be real healings from Reiki (*if* they last and are not merely a placebo), they do not come from God. Remember that the Devil can mimic the works of God and even transform himself into an "angel of light" (see Ex 7:10–11, 20–22; Rv 13:11–14; 2 Cor 11:14). The Book of Revelation makes it clear that those in the service of the Devil were allowed to do miracles and great signs, but the great signs were not from God. This is why we need to discern properly.

25. "How Does Reiki Work?," International Center for Reiki Training, accessed September 26, 2019, https://www.reiki.org/faq/howdoesreikiwork.html.

26. Susan Brinkmann, "Exorcist: Yoga/Reiki Can Be Point of Entry for Demons," *Women of Grace* (blog), August 28, 2015, accessed September 26, 2019, http://ht.ly/Rv8KX. See also "Is Reiki Dangerous?," Quora.com, accessed September 26, 2019, https://www.quora.com/Is-Reiki-dangerous.

27. Noonan, *Ransomed from Darkness*, 42, 44, 92.

28. Committee on Doctrine, "Guidelines for Evaluating Reiki as an Alternative Therapy," United States Conference of Catholic Bishops, accessed September 26, 2019, http://www.usccb

.org/_cs_upload/8092_1.pdf.

CHAPTER 7

1. Father Thomas Keating had many interreligious dialogues with Hindus and Buddhists, which led him to conduct week-long Zen Buddhist retreats with his own Catholic monks for nearly a decade. Keating sought to merge these other religious traditions with his own Catholic faith. The result was "Centering Prayer."

2. Congregation for the Doctrine of the Faith (CDF), "Letter to the Bishops of the Catholic Church on Some Aspects of Christian Meditation," October 15, 1989, accessed September 26, 2019, http://www.vatican.va/roman_curia/congregations/cfaith /documents/rc_con_cfaith_doc_19891015_meditazione -cristiana_en.html.

3. Thomas Keating, *Open Mind, Open Heart*, 20th-anniversary ed. (New York: Continuum International, 2006), 158.

4. "United in Prayer Day," *Newsletter of Contemplative Outreach of Northern San Diego* 4, no. 2 (May 2009), http://consd.org /wp-content/uploads/2009/12/May_2009_newsletter.pdf.

5. Many New Age practitioners utilize this line of thinking regarding the divine Self. Father Basil Pennington, cofounder of Centering Prayer, devoted an entire book to this topic: *True Self / False Self: Unmasking the Spirit Within*.

6. A similar philosophy, if not the same in essence, is known as panentheism, which teaches that God is in everything and everything is in God (another Hindu concept). Therefore, even though we are not God, we are still divine and one with him and his essence, because we are a part or extension of his being. This is still a distorted New Age understanding of God.

7. Pontifical Council for Culture and Pontifical Council for Religious Dialogue, *Jesus Christ, the Bearer of the Water of Life: A Christian Reflection on the "New Age,"* accessed September 26, 2019, http://www.vatican.va/roman_curia/pontifical_councils /interelg/documents/rc_pc_interelg_doc_20030203_new-age _en.html.

8. Ibid.

9. Keating, *Open Mind, Open Heart*, 36.

10. CDF, "Some Aspects of Christian Meditation."

11. Thomas Dubay, SM, *Prayer Primer: Igniting a Fire Within* (Ann Arbor, MI: Servant, 2002), 155.

12. Thomas Dubay, SM, *Fire Within: St. Teresa of Avila, St. John of the Cross and the Gospel — On Prayer* (San Francisco: Ignatius Press, 1989), 86.

13. Saint John of the Cross talks extensively about different prayer experiences, including both dryness and dry desires, in his book *Dark Night of the Soul*.

14. Pontifical Council for Culture and Pontifical Council for Religious Dialogue, *Jesus Christ, the Bearer of the Water of Life*.

Chapter 8

1. Don Richard Riso with Russ Hudson, *The Wisdom of the Enneagram* (New York: Bantam Books, 1999), 10.

2. Father Mitch Pacwa, S.J., *Catholics and the New Age* (Ann Arbor, MI: Servant, 1992), 100.

3. Riso and Hudson, *The Wisdom of the Enneagram*, 20.

4. Ibid., 21–22.

5. Pacwa, *Catholics and the New Age*.

6. Ibid., 112.

7. Ibid., 114.

8. "Enneagram Prayer of Gratitude," Facebook, posted June 9, 2010, accessed September 26, 2019, https://www.facebook.com/notes/world-gratitude /enneagram-prayer-of-gratitude/399114314226/.

9. Mitchell Pacwa, SJ, "Tell Me Who I Am, O Enneagram," Christian Research Institute, June 9, 2009, accessed September 26, 2019, https://www.equip.org/article /tell-me-who-i-am-o-enneagram/.

10. Pontifical Council for Culture and Pontifical Council for Religious Dialogue, *Jesus Christ, the Bearer of the Water of Life*.

11. Joshua J. Mark, "Labyrinth," *Ancient History Encyclopedia*,

published April 18, 2018, accessed August 9, 2019, https://www
.ancient.eu/Labyrinth/.

12. "A Recognized Cultural Creative," LaurenArtress.com,
accessed September 26, 2019, https://www.laurenartress.com/
spiritual-pioneer/.

13. Ibid.

14. Susan Brinkmann, OCDS, *Learn to Discern: Is It Christian or New Age? Labyrinths* (Oldsmar, FL: Simon Peter Press,
2008), 18.

15. Ibid., 19.

16. "Our Labyrinths," Grace Cathedral, accessed September 26,
2019, https://gracecathedral.org/our-labyrinths/.

17. Ibid.

CHAPTER 9

1. Robert E. Kennedy, *Zen Spirit, Christian Spirit: The Place of
Zen in Christian Life* (New York: Continuum International,
1995), 28.

2. Ibid., 32.

3. Ruben L. F. Habito, *Healing Breath: Zen for Christians and
Buddhists in a Wounded World* (Boston: Wisdom Publications,
2006), 28–29.

4. "Maharishi Mahesh Yogi, Meditation Teacher," Transcendental Meditation News and More, June 12, 2105, accessed
September 26, 2019, https://tmhome.com/books-videos
/maharishi-mahesh-yogi-tm/.

5. Ibid.

6. "Transcending = the Highest Human Experience," *Transcendental Meditation*, accessed September 26, 2019, https://tran-
scendental-meditation.be/the-highest-human-experience/.

7. Kevin McSpadden, "You Now Have a Shorter Attention Span
Than a Goldfish," *Time*, May 14, 2015, accessed September 26,
2019, https://time.com/3858309/attention-spans-goldfish. See
also Tore Vind Jensen, "Abundance of Information Narrows
Our Collective Attention Span," DTU, April 15, 2019,

https://www.dtu.dk/english/news/nyhed?id=246BBED3-8683-4012-A294-20DB7F0015F4.

8. Dr. Gregory Bottaro, *The Mindful Catholic* (North Palms Beach, FL: Beacon Publishing, 2018), 19.

9. Jeny Liu, *Discover Feng Shui: Companion Booklet* (n.p.: New Feng Shui Concepts, 2000), 24–25.

10. Noonan, *Ransomed*, 138.

11. Karl Keating, "Crystal Craziness," Catholic.com, April 1, 1990, accessed September 26, 2019, https://www.catholic.com /magazine/print-edition/crystal-craziness.

12. Neil Gumenick, "The Spirits of the Points: The Large Intestine Meridian," *Acupuncture Today* 12, no. 10 (October 2011), https://www.acupuncturetoday.com/mpacms/at/article .php?id=32466.

13. Steven Novella, "False Claims for Acupuncture," *Science-Based Medicine*, December 6, 2017, accessed September 26, 2019, https://sciencebasedmedicine.org/false-claims-for-acupuncture/.

14. Stephen Barrett, M.D., "Be Wary of Acupuncture, Qigong, and 'Chinese Medicine,' " Quackwatch, revised January 12, 2011, accessed September 26, 2019, https://www.quackwatch .org/01QuackeryRelatedTopics/acu.html.

15. "Acupuncture: In Depth," National Center for Complementary and Integrative Health, accessed September 26, 2019, https://nccih.nih.gov/health/acupuncture/introduction#hed2.

16. Marcia Montenegro, "Yin and Yang: Getting into the Flow," Christian Answers for the New Age, accessed September 26, 2019, http://www.christiananswersforthenewage.org/Articles_YinYang.html.

17. Ibid.

18. Jayaram V, "Hinduism and the Belief of Rebirth," Hinduwebsite.com, accessed September 26, 2019, https://www.hinduwebsite.com/reincarnation.asp.

19. Ibid.

20. Ibid.

21. Pontifical Council for Culture and Pontifical Council for Religious Dialogue, *Jesus Christ, the Bearer of the Water of Life*.

22. Carol Bowman, "Experience Your Past Lives," Carol Bowman, Past Life Therapy, accessed September 26, 2019, https://www.carolbowman.com/past-life-regression/.

23. Ibid.

24. Noonan, *Ransomed*, 41–42.

25. Stephen Barrett, M.D., "Past-Life Therapy," in "Mental Help: Procedures to Avoid," Quackwatch, accessed September 26, 2019, https://www.quackwatch.org/01QuackeryRelatedTopics/mentserv.html#pastlife.

26. Gabriel Andrade, "Is Past Life Regression Therapy Ethical?," *Journal of Ethics and History of Medicine* 10, no. 11 (December 2017), https://www.ncbi.nlm.nih.gov/pmc/articles/PMC5797677/.

27. Robin Cathleen Coale, M.A., L.P.C., "What Is a Shaman?," Sacred Shamanic Healing, accessed September 26, 2019, http://www.sacredshamanichealing.com/10-Shamanism.html.

28. "Shaman," *Merriam-Webster Dictionary*, accessed September 26, 2019, https://www.merriam-webster.com/dictionary/shaman.

29. Ibid.

30. Mircea Eliade and Vilmos Diószegi, "Shamanism," *Encyclopedia Britannica*, accessed September 26, 2019, https://www.britannica.com/topic/shamanism.

31. Mark Oppenheimer, "A Company Aims to Put Good Karma and Energy Close at Hand," *New York Times*, March 28, 2014, https://www.nytimes.com/2014/03/29/us/seeking-good-karma-a-company-aims-to-put-it-close-at-hand.html?_r=1&referer=.

32. Ibid.

Conclusion

1. Catholic Review, "Catholics Need Solid Preaching, Not Fluff," Archdiocese of Baltimore, January 19, 2012, accessed

September 26, 2019, https://www.archbalt.org/catholics-need-solid-preaching-not-fluff/.

2. Thomas E. Woods, *How the Catholic Church Built Western Civilization* (Washington, DC: Regnery Publishing, 2005), 47.

Bibliography

Books Cited and Recommended for Further Learning

Amorth, Gabriele. *An Exorcist Tells His Story.* San Francisco: Ignatius Press, 1999.

———. *An Exorcist, More Stories.* San Francisco: Ignatius Press, 2002.

Arnold, Matthew. *Overcoming the New Age Movement.* Sycamore, IL: Catholic Lighthouse Media, 2008. CD-ROM.

Benkovic, Johnnette S. *The New Age Counterfeit.* Goleta, CA: Queenship Publishing, 1993.

Bottaro, Gregory. The Mindful Catholic. North Palm Beach, FL: Beacon Publishing, 2018.

Brinkmann, Susan, OCDS. *Learn to Discern: Is it Christian or New Age?* Oldsmar, FL: St. Peter's Press, 2008.

Carey, Ann. *Sisters in Crisis.* San Francisco: Ignatius Press, 1997.

Catechism of the Catholic Church. New York: Doubleday, 1994.

Congregation for the Doctrine of Faith. "Declaration *Dominus Iesus* on the Unicity and Salvific Universality of Jesus Christ and the Church." vatican.va, August 6, 2000.

———. "Letter to the Bishops of the Catholic Church on Some Aspects of Christian Meditation." vatican.va, October 15, 1989.

———. "Notification Concerning the Writings of Father Anthony De Mello, SJ." vatican.va, June 24, 1998.

———. "Notification on the Book *Toward a Christian Theology of Religious Pluralism* (Orbis Books: Maryknoll, New York 1997) by Father Jacques Dupuis, SJ." vatican.va, July 24,

2001.

———. "Notification on the Works of Father Jon Sobrino, SJ." Vatican.va, November 26, 2006.

Dreher, John D. "The Dangers of Centering Prayer." Catholic. com, November 1, 1997.

Dubay, Thomas, S.M. *A Fire Within: St. Teresa of Avila, St. John of the Cross and the Gospel — On Prayer.* San Francisco: Ignatius Press, 1989.

———. *Prayer Primer: Igniting a Fire Within.* Ann Arbor, MI: Servant, 2002.

Encyclopedia Britannica. "Samadhi." Britannica.com. Accessed November 9, 2018. https://www.britannica.com/topic /samadhi-Indian-philosophy.

England, Randy. *Unicorn in the Sanctuary.* Rockford, IL: TAN Books, 1990.

Francis de Sales. *Introduction to the Devout Life.* 400th-anniversary ed. Point Roberts, WA: Eremitical Press, 2009.

Hardon, John A., SJ. *Pocket Catholic Dictionary.* New York: Doubleday, 1985.

Kilpatrick, William Kirk. *The Emperor's New Clothes.* Westchester, IL: Crossway Books, 1985.

Lebar, James J. *Cults, Sects, and the New Age Movement.* Huntington, IN: Our Sunday Visitor, 1989.

Hauke, Manfred. *God or Goddess?* San Francisco: Ignatius Press, 1993.

McInerny, Ralph M. *What Went Wrong with Vatican II.* Manchester, NH: Sophia Institute Press, 1998.

McKenna, Briege, OSC. *Miracles Do Happen: God Can Do the Impossible.* Ann Arbor, MI: Servant, 2002.

Noonan, Moira. *Ransomed from Darkness.* El Sobrante, CA: North Bay Books, 2005.

Pacwa, Mitch, SJ. *Catholics and the New Age.* Ann Arbor, MI: Servant, 1992.

Pollok, Robert. *World Religions.* NY: Fall River Press, 2008.

Rivera Carrera, Archbishop Norberto. "A Call to Vigilance:

Pastoral Instruction on New Age." EWTN.com, January 7, 1996.

Steichen, Donna. *Ungodly Rage: The Hidden Face of Catholic Feminism*. San Francisco: Ignatius Press, 1992.

Teresa of Ávila. *Interior Castle*. New York: Doubleday, 1989.

United States Conference of Catholic Bishops, Committee on Doctrine. "Guidelines for Evaluating Reiki as an Alternative Therapy." USCCB, March 25, 2009.

Vanderpool Film Productions. *In the Grip of Evil*. WINStar Home Entertainment, 1998.

Valdéz, Jorge. *Coming Clean*. Colorado Springs, CO: Water-Brook Press, 1999.

Whalen, William J. *Strange Gods*. Huntington, IN: Our Sunday Visitor, 1981.

Woods, Thomas E. *How the Catholic Church Built Western Civilization*. Washington, DC: Regnery, 2005.

Books Cited and *Not* Recommended

Boon, Brooke. *Holy Yoga: Exercise for the Christian Body and Soul*. New York: Faith Words, 2007.

Byrne, Rhonda. *The Secret*. New York: Atria Books, 2006.

Chopra, Deepak. *The Third Jesus: The Christ We Cannot Ignore*. New York: Three Rivers Press, 2008.

Collins, Terah Kathryn. *Feng Shui: Personal Paradise Cards*. Carlsbad, CA: Hay House, 2001.

Ferguson, Marylin. *The Aquarian Conspiracy: Personal and Social Transformation in the 1980s*. Los Angeles: J. P. Tarcher, 1980.

Fox, Matthew. *The Coming of the Cosmic Christ*. New York: HarperCollins Publishers, 1988.

Habito, Ruben, L. F. *Healing Breath: Zen for Christians and Buddhists in a Wounded World*. Boston, MA: Wisdom Publications, 2006.

Harris, Maria. *Dance of the Spirit: The Seven Steps of Women's Spirituality*. New York: Bantam Books, 1989.

Iyengar, B. K. S. *Yoga: The Path to Holistic Health*. New York: Dorling Kindersley, 2001.

———. *Light on Yoga*. New York: Schocken Books, 1976.

Jampolsky, Gerald, G., M.D. *Love Is Letting Go of Fear*. Berkeley, CA: Celestial Arts, 1979.

Keating, Thomas. *Journey to the Center*. New York: Crossroad Publishing, 1999.

———. *Open Mind, Open Heart*. 20th-anniversary ed. New York: Continuum International, 2006.

Kennedy, Robert E. *Zen Spirit, Christian Spirit: The Place of Zen in Christian Life*. New York: Continuum International, 1995.

Liu, Jenny. *Discover Feng Shui: DVD Companion Booklet*. New Feng Shui Concepts, 2000.

Lübeck, Walter. *The Complete Reiki Handbook*. Twin Lakes, WI: Lotus Light Shangri-La, 1998.

Lübeck, Walter, Frank Arjava Petter, William Lee Rand, and Christine M. Grimm. *The Spirit of Reiki: The Complete Handbook of the Reiki System*. Twin Lakes, WI: Lotus Press, 2003.

Morwood, Michael. *Is Jesus God? Finding Our Faith*. New York: Crossroad Publishing, 2001.

Myss, Caroline. *Entering the Castle*. New York: Free Press, 2007.

Paul, Russill. *Jesus in the Lotus: The Mystical Doorway between Christianity and Yogic Spirituality*. Novato, CA: New World Library, 2009.

Pennington, M. Basil. *True Self /False Self: Unmasking the Spirit Within*. New York: Crossroad Publishing, 2000.

Riso, Don Richard, with Russ Hudson. *The Wisdom of the Enneagram*. New York: Bantam Books, 1999.

Rohr, Richard. *The Naked Now: Learning to See as the Mystics See*. New York: Crossroad Publishing , 2009.

Rosen, Richard. *Yoga FAQ: Almost Everything You Need to Know about Yoga — from Asanas to Yamas*. Boulder, CO: Shambhala Publications, 2017.

Schucman, Helen. *A Course in Miracles: Combined Volume*. 2nd ed. New York: Penguin, 1996.

Singleton, Mark. *Yoga Body: The Origins of Modern Posture Practice*. New York: Oxford University Press, 2010.

Taylor, Sarah McFarlan. *Green Sisters*. Harvard, MA: Harvard University Press, 2007.

Thompson, Vicky. *The Jesus Path*. Boston, MA: Red Wheel/ Weiser, 2003.

Tolle, Eckhart. *A New Earth: Awakening to Your Life's Purpose*. New York: First Plume Printing, 2005.

———. *The Power of NOW: A Guide to Spiritual Enlightenment*. Novato, CA: New World Library, 1999.

Usui, Dr. Mikao, and Frank Arjava Petter. *The Original Reiki Handbook of Dr. Mikao Usui*. Twin Lakes, WI: Lotus Press, 2011.

Walsch, Neale Donald. *Conversations with God: An Uncommon Dialogue*. vol. 1. New York: G. P. Putnam's Sons, 1995.

———. *Conversations with God: An Uncommon Dialogue*. vol. 2. Charlottesville, VA: Hampton Roads, 1997.

Williamson, Marianne. *The Gift of Change*. New York: Harper San Francisco, 2004.

Willis, Jennifer Schwamm. *The Joy of Yoga*. New York: Marlowe and Company, 2002.

About the Author

BRYAN MERCIER is a professional Catholic speaker, radio host, and author. He has spoken to adults and teens for nearly twenty years and has been aired on TV and radio, including EWTN. Bryan is a graduate of Franciscan University and holds a master's degree in theology from Holy Apostles College.